# The Real Matrix - Christ vs Satan: The Second Coming of Christ

## Lucifer Rebellion

### Trinity Royal

Copyright © 2022 by Trinity Royal

Legal Notice: This book is copyright protected. It is only for personal use. You cannot amend, distribute, sell, use, quote, or paraphrase any part, or the content within this book, without the consent of the author or publisher, except as permitted by U.S. copyright law. Under no circumstances will any blame or legal responsibility be held against the publisher, or author, for any damages, reparation, or monetary loss due to the information contained within this book, either directly or indirectly.

Disclaimer Notice: Please note the information contained within this document is for educational and entertainment purposes only. All effort has been executed to present accurate, up-to-date, reliable, and complete information. No warranties of any kind are declared or implied. Readers acknowledge that the author is not engaged in the rendering of legal, financial, medical, or professional advice. The content within this book has been derived from various sources. Please consult a licensed professional before attempting any techniques outlined in this book. The reader agrees that under no circumstances is the author responsible for any losses, direct or indirect, that are incurred as a result of the use of the information contained within this document, including, but not limited to, errors, omissions, or inaccuracies.

Library of Congress Control Number: 2022917136 | Digital ISBN: 978-1-957681-10-8

## Table of Contents

Free books to our readers ................................ 1

Introduction ................................................... 3

Lucifer Rebellion - War in Heaven Summary 8

Why Christ Came to Planet Earth ................ 18

First Coming Mission Result - Halt the march of Darkness ........................................................ 29

Follow the White Rabbit ................................ 38

The Stage is Set - Final Battle for Planet Earth has Begun ........................................................ 50

Second Coming of Christ ................................ 56

Conclusion ....................................................... 64

Thank You ....................................................... 66

Scripture verses Related to War in Heaven from Bible ................................................................. 67

Preview from Book - Lucifer Rebellion book1: Clarion Call from GOD to all the Angels in Heaven ............................................................ 71

Preview from book - Son of Man becomes Son of God .................................................................. 80

Lucifer Rebellion. Christ vs. Satan – Final Battle for Earth Has Begun ............................................ 98

Christ & Demons - Unseen Realms of Darkness ................................................................... 100

Son of Man becomes Son of God. ................ 101

SOS - Save yOur Soul ..................................... 102

Welcome to Heaven. ...................................... 103

Your Life in Heaven ....................................... 104

From Suffering to Healing ............................. 105

Dark Night of the Soul .................................. 106

Free books to our readers ............................. 107

References ..................................................... 108

About Author ................................................ 110

# Free books to our readers

**War in Heaven came to Earth. Satan Rebellion:**

https://dl.bookfunnel.com/ea12ys3dmk

**Your Life in Heaven:**

https://dl.bookfunnel.com/vg451qpuzs

"And there was war in heaven: Michael and his angels fought against the dragon; and the dragon fought and his angels, And prevailed not; neither was their place found any more in heaven.

And the great dragon was cast out, that old serpent, called the Devil, and Satan, which deceiveth the whole world: he was cast out into the earth, and his angels were cast out with him."

- [Revelation] 12:7-9

# Introduction

All the major religions of the world including Christianity, Islam, Judaism, Hinduism, and Buddhism agree on one critical fact – there is Heaven and Hell, God and His adversary, and Light and Dark, both are opposites. The adversary is called by different names including Satan, Shaytan, Iblis, and Lucifer. All religions also agree both factions are powerful adversaries and that Human beings are part of this epic battle. Most of the details in all of the scriptural texts are either high-level or sketchy at best; there is no explanation. This is subject to different interpretations and confusion among theologians.

The Holy Bible when seen through the lens of history has more info comparatively than other religious scriptures about the war in heaven but this also falls short. My sincere attempt in this book is to shine a light on this great epic war that has origins beyond planet Earth space and time. The reader will travel back in time to when Lucifer Rebellion began. We will see what exactly happened at that time, and since then, and its effects on this present day.

To my knowledge, this is the first time this level of information is being presented to Humanity. Because it is TIME. The final bell has rung, and the climatic battle is at hand. You will see why this is so later in the book.

The Matrix was one of the most popular movies ever released in the history of the industry. Just about anyone, anywhere in the world, can describe its basic plot to you: The hero, Neo, an ordinary computer programmer, somehow knows that something is off in the world he inhabits. He meets Morpheus, takes the red pill, and realizes that his world is an illusion—one created by sentient machines to enslave humanity so that humans could be used as a power source by malevolent mechanisms. By breaking free of the matrix, the illusory world, Neo could lead his fellow man to freedom and liberation.

Now think of a different scene, one not portrayed in that movie or any other. Imagine one army on the right side of a great galactic battlefield—a mighty host of creatures of all shapes and sizes, hoisting aloft a banner consisting of three concentric unbroken azure circles (representing the good government of the entire universe) on a white background. At the head of this army of Light is the greatest religious figure we know of—Jesus Christ. Opposing him, streaming from the left side of the galactic battlefield, are legions upon legions of Dark creatures, as varied as their Light counterparts but wreathed in shadow and ill omen. The most notorious demon in history, Satan, is leading them, carrying a banner displaying a red circle on an equally white background with a solid black circle in its center.

Surrounding these great armies is a galactic host of trillions upon trillions of creatures. Not only from our galaxy but from across the entire universe; they are watching the two forces of Light and Dark go head-to-head with each other. At the very center of the struggle between them is a single little ball of blue and green: Our home planet, earth. And this battle is the very climax of a struggle that has been going on for far, far longer than any of us has been alive. This battle takes place at the 11th minute of the 11th hour of the great war between these elemental forces, with the Earth and Universe at stake.

The armies cannot fight on, or interfere with earth directly on their own. But the residents of the earth have free will and can petition the warriors of both sides for help, depending on their freely made choices. The two sides are fighting for the souls of humans and will lead them to either destruction or ascension to Heaven.

Questions this Book Will Answer

Book-1:

- What is Lucifer's Rebellion? When and why did the Lucifer rebellion start?
- What is Lucifer/Satan's agenda?
- How did the 'Fall' happen?
- What is the ONE reason Dark and Light are fighting for on planet Earth?
- Why did God have to make a clarion call to all the angels for humanity's assistance?
- How the Dark and Light are fighting and what is the evidence?
- What is the reason for the bestowal of the Creator of the Universe on Earth - Jesus Christ?
- What exactly happened between Christ and Satan in the wilderness on Mt. Hermon?

- What is the evidence that we are almost at the climatic battle point, at the 11th hour?
- How do dark forces operate to keep you stuck in this Veil of separation (spiritual Matrix)? How do you know or even recognize this?
- How to free yourself from the Matrix?

Book-2:

- What did Christ accomplish in His First Coming?
- What is the unfinished business leading to Second Coming?
- What is on the agenda for Christ's Second Coming? (hint: It is more than rapture)
- What can planet Earth expect from Christ's Second coming?
- When can we expect the Second Coming event?
- How long do we have? When is this epic war going to end?

Hmm…these are really good questions. Do you agree? This book will answer all these and much more.

This could revolutionize the way you see life.

"God's laser focus is on Earth and humanity; this is where all the action of the universe is. Big shots from across the universe are

gathered and watching the chess games being played by Light and Dark armies. This is our current reality, not fiction." – Trinity Royal

# Lucifer Rebellion - War in Heaven Summary

"Spiritual warfare is very real. There's a furious, fierce, and ferocious battle raging in the realm of the spirit between the forces of God and the forces of evil. Warfare happens every day, all the time. Whether you believe it or not, you are on a battlefield. You are in warfare." — Pedro Okoro

It is time to travel in time to the origins of the war in heaven itself. Records of this time are scattered and fragmentary–even in the Bible, the book of Urantia, or others. We may not have the full story and might never have it. Much of the history and physical evidence for what I am about to tell you has been intentionally destroyed by a side in the conflict. But countless hours of research and a degree of "insider knowledge" have allowed me to give you the basics.

Now, God did not want to be alone, so he filled the many, many planets in this universe with creatures of his own. Some were just plants and animals, but many of them were sentient beings who could receive God's love and who thus, love him back. God did the same across multitudes and multitudes of other universes and planets of existence. Some universes were higher than others, and all of them (and all the residents of all the planets within them) had the goal of growing closer and closer to God across many lifetimes to reach Paradise - the universe very closest to God. To help the various lower creatures ascend, God created immaterial spiritual messengers from Paradise—known as angels or by many other names—to pass down wisdom and advice in attaining Godliness.

Just about every religion offers an account of the creation of the world. The Old Testament speaks of God separating the light and darkness and creating the heavens and the earth in seven days, and the Muslim holy text, the Quran, agrees with that account. All three of the Abrahamic faiths also speak of a great flood blotting out life on earth due to man's iniquity, and similar ideas can be seen in even polytheistic religions.

Plato, the Greek thinker who was arguably the father of the Western philosophical tradition in general, wrote in the Phaedo about how one's soul could be refined throughout lifetimes to eventually reach union with the Greek gods and how it never truly dies even though the body might. But there are Dark forces in addition to divine ones who are interested in our immortal souls. Some, as in the Abrahamic traditions, call him Lucifer, Satan, or Shaitan. The idea of a "Dark Lord" is prominent even in our entertainment and fantasy stories, like Sauron in The Lord of the Rings or Smith in The Matrix . All of these are echoes of an important spiritual truth. This chapter will describe the leader of those Dark forces and what he has in store for us in reality.

Origin of the Rebellion

Lucifer

God created Lucifer as a unique being in that he was an Angel, the most beautiful angel of all created, and he had free will, and the ability to make his own decisions and act on them. The original Aramaic name Lucifer translates to Morning Star. Lucifer is mentioned in the Bible only two times but is said to have sat at God's side and worshipped him and loved him deeply. Lucifer was regarded as the wisest, greatest, and most beautiful angel in all of creation, having virtually no equal with only God being his superior. He is described as the most beautiful and the brightest angel in existence and regarded as the perfection of beauty and wisdom. 'His beauty exceeded all other angels in heaven to the point where a mere glance would make anyone go mad from the sheer beauty and power. 'He is noted to have six colossal whitish gold wings, that almost looked like made of light. According to the old testament, when Lucifer was in heaven his clothing was adorned with many precious stones, all beautifully crafted for him and set in the finest gold.

Christ

Christ, the Creator of our Universe is the Son of God. Christ is viewed as the field commander of all the 'Heavenly hosts and the strongest angel in all of Heaven and creation.' Both Christ and Lucifer looked like twins of great power and glory. Both Christ and Lucifer had complete free will and continued to aid in the creation of the celestial bodies across the universe along with their Father. Christ is the name of the Creator of the Universe. Michael is the title. Christ Michael and Christ names are used interchangeably. Both refer to the same being.

The War in Heaven

The Bible mentions that God created angels to worship him and they encircle him with praise and song eternally. These angels do not have free will and exist only to worship and praise God. Another group was created called Arch Angels and although smaller in number they had power and carried out God's wishes. They delivered messages, intervened in disputes or problems, and could decide to take an action while doing this work but always one that was directed or approved by God.

Lucifer's Pride

Due to Lucifer being the favored Angel, God would reveal to him His plans for the creation. The more God told Lucifer His plans, the more problems Lucifer began to see. His thoughts began to stray from what his Father desired. Eventually, it led to a series of heated arguments between God and Lucifer. Lucifer started to question God and only grow infuriated by God's answers ending in God admonishing Lucifer each time. Whenever Lucifer would leave, he would deduce and soon realize that everything and everyone would be under the shadow of God's hand, living and acting the way God wants and chooses for them to live and act. This became known as "predestination." Lucifer grew heavily opposed to this concept of "predestination" which involves the destiny of all being under God's will and command.

Lucifer's pride began to overtake him and grew more rebellious against his Father. It soon led to Lucifer becoming dissatisfied with following God. Lucifer did not like to be under God's authority. He did not believe that anyone should be above him or be in control of him. According to Lucifer, God is growing senile, and God is not worthy to sit on the throne. He wanted to be like God and he wanted his own creation. He wanted complete autonomy and free will. Lucifer's paranoia made him see God as a tyrannical ruler and declared that no one should control other lives and fate, instead, they should be free agents who have control over their choices and actions. He then proclaimed that he would rule in God's stead to rid the concept of predestination.

"You (referring to Lucifer) were the anointed guardian cherub. I placed you; you were on the holy mountain of God in the midst of the stones of fire you walked." – Ezekiel 8:14.

Lucifer finally launched his "Declaration of Liberty". Lucifer declared before all the heavenly hosts, and legions of angels, that self/government should be the law of the universe and all the solar systems should be freed from the Universal Father's yoke' and rule themselves. However, he also proclaimed that he was the "friend of men and angels" and "God of liberty."

"I will ascend into heaven, I will exalt my throne above the starts of God; I will also sit on the mount of the congregation on the farthest sides of the north; I will also ascend the heights of the clouds, I will be like the Most High." – Isaiah 14:13-14

He proposed a new Creation concept. Lucifer sincerely believed that with his new creation, he could enhance and fasten spiritual growth compared to the current process of step-by-step evolution under God's rule. Lucifer wanted to be the creator of souls. He thought that by using laboratory methods, machine intelligence, and his creative abilities, he could give a portion of himself to create new souls that can evolve faster with higher intelligence, that the current way under God's ruling, which is a slow, long, and methodical process of evolution.

Additionally, Lucifer also proposed the concept of "karma", which is cause and effect. What you sow you reap. He sincerely believed that this will help the souls to learn and evolve faster. As talented and charming as he is, he was able to sell his concept of new creation and evolution to 1/3rd of the angels in heaven.

"And war broke out in Heaven. (Christ) Michael and His angels fought with the dragon2 and the dragon and his angels fought." – Revelations 48

With 1/3rd of the Angels, Lucifer waged a full-fledged war against God. Lucifer had recruited his trump card "Satan" a high angel to be his second in command and Beelzebub as his lieutenant.

Satan

Before his fall from Heaven, Satan was more noble, just, and fair but strict and firm. He was an exalted cherub and thus had great pride over his power and position. Satan is a powerful heavenly being, so much so that he was specifically chosen by Lucifer to be his ultimate trump card during the war in heaven. Next to both

Lucifer and Christ, he is the most powerful angel created by God. After his fall from grace also, he wields immeasurable supernatural power although fairly weakened after being confined in Hell. However, Satan should not be underestimated as he remains the most powerful entity in all of Hell and Earth. He is praised for being the second most powerful being only next to Lucifer himself and rivaling Lucifer as well. He was strong enough to defeat an armada of angels and also take on Christ. He is regarded as a huge threat to Heaven and even directly challenges God.

The immensity of his power is evident when he imbues his loyal followers with great demonic power allowing them to go head-to-head with other mighty angelic beings. He is also known to be an accomplished master in the art of black magic and has incredible knowledge in all manners of spells, having no superior other than possibly Lucifer. After he fell into the Abyss and emerged from the crater, he renounced his angelic name and went by the title of "Satan" which means Adversary. He emerged as a new being and one that would be against all that God had created. He chose the name "Satan" as a declaration that he will be the ultimate enemy of mankind. In agreement with Lucifer and Beelzebub, he wants to prove to God that, God's greatest creation of Humankind is not as great as He proclaims to His angels.

With 1/3rd of the angels, Lucifer waged a full-fledged war against God and Christ.

"And there was war in heaven: Michael and his angels fought against the dragon; and the dragon fought and his angels, And prevailed not; neither was their place found any more in heaven. And the great dragon was cast out, that old serpent, called the

Devil, and Satan, which deceiveth the whole world: he was cast out into the earth, and his angels were cast out with him." - [Revelation 12:7-9]

Christ defeated Lucifer and then banished him and his followers from Heaven. And so did Lucifer Fall from grace with the utmost tragedy, horror, dismay, and terror.

He was cast to the Earth, and his angels were cast out with him. – Revelations 12:9

"And I beheld Satan fall as lightning from heaven." - Luke 10:18

The Book of Isaiah also records this event -

"How you are fallen from heaven, O Lucifer, son of the morning! How you are cut down to the ground, you who weakened the nations! For you have said in your heart: 'I will ascend into heaven, I will exalt my throne above the stars of God; I will also sit on the mount of the congregation on the farthest sides of the north; I will ascend above the heights of the clouds, I will be like the Most High'" (Isaiah 14:12-14).

# Why Christ Came to Planet Earth

In a universe as vast as ours, with all of its solar systems and galaxies, why would the Divine take such an interest in a small planet orbiting an unremarkable star at the very edge of the Milky Way?

The Order of the Universe

The Bible is certainly one of the greatest books ever written. Christians obviously find it holy, but even members of other faiths, or no faith at all, can acknowledge the power of its moral teachings and the insight it provides into transcendent reality.

As the Bible teaches, there is only one supreme God, creator of humanity, Earth itself, and the heavens above, all the stars we see in the night sky, and many more beyond. So great is God's power that he did not create a single planet, but many thousands upon thousands—so very many that human beings can scarcely conceive of such a humongous multitude. In His infinite wisdom, in order to best minister to the innumerable beings who need His guidance, God will sometimes distribute His power in the form of spiritual servants to directly oversee galaxies, then solar systems, and then individual planets with life on them.

However, while the Bible concentrates primarily on God's interactions with human beings on Earth, we are not the only ones He is concerned with. Many of the stars we see are orbited by planets, and on some of those planets, life evolved, just like it did on Earth (with Genesis being understood as an allegory for God's concern with sapient life specifically). Intelligent creatures with souls like human beings arose on an even smaller number of those planets. Though such aliens are naturally very different from us in physical shape, they are also capable of language, reasoning, and empathy for other living things, which makes them similar to us spiritually, and explains why God is concerned with them as well. In return, all the wisest and most enlightened inhabited planets of the universe also recognize and worship God, giving thanks and praise to Him in a multitude of their own ways.

By separating Himself into emissaries, and having those divine emissaries struggle through the responsibilities of overseeing galaxies, and planets, and occasionally even incarnating themselves physically to live amongst the mortals they rule, God shares the joy and pain of His creations, and thus the glory of their self-improvement as well, which does not contradict but enhances and deepens the already-existing glory of His divine nature, personality, and mode of existence.

Needless to say, it is very easy to understand how all of this would apply to Christ's appearance on Earth. God and His emissaries, being wise and caring, know they have to incarnate within a world in a material universe at precisely the right time and place, and in precisely the right social context (given the individual development of that world in terms of culture, religion, and understanding of God and morality, socioeconomic factors, and so on) in order to leave the most positive impact.

For Earth, that time was 0 A.D., in the context of the Jewish people living under Roman rule in the Middle East. As the analysis of the Old Testament, we have performed earlier illustrates, the prophets and sages of Jewish history had made great strides in understanding God's will, His greatness, and the moral tenets He wanted His creations to uphold. Although cloaked in myth and allegory appropriate for a species that had not yet, at the time, created advanced science, Jewish teaching affirmed the omni-benevolence, uniqueness, and oneness of the Universal Father. The Old Testament also contained many powerful moral messages to ensure its adherents stayed on the right path: admonitions to protect orphans and widows, care for the poor, be honest and forthright in your dealings with everyone (even your enemies), and how God's mercy would always be extended to anyone who asked for it (NIV, Exodus 22:22-27).

Now, as the Bible also states, by the time Christ was born people had started to lose sight of these teachings, so to purify them and bring the people back to the most important basics (so to speak), it was just the right moment for God Himself to direct one of His emissaries to do the job personally. Also, through the strength of that emissary's preaching and teaching skills, the noble moral teachings the Jewish people had refined throughout the centuries could be spread to humanity in general through the Roman Empire, which was the largest and most far-reaching in the world at the time.

Who, exactly, was that emissary? Before He was Jesus, this individuation of the Universal Father's power was Christ (also known as Christ Michael in the higher levels of the Universe).

The Importance of Earth

You might also be wondering: Why Earth, specifically? After all, given how vast our universe is, even if its creator, there are many millions of worlds in our universe. Why did He not incarnate (or, as the technical language goes, proceed through a Bestowal) on one of those? The answer has to do with what makes human beings particularly important in the grand scheme of things.

Darkness is concentrated on Earth. What happens on Earth has ripple effects across the Universe.

As we have seen before, the dark forces have been quarantined to this sector of the galaxy, with Earth being the epicenter. Planet

Earth is quarantined or locked-down to arrest the spread of the virus of darkness.

In higher realms, planet Earth is called "The Planet of Sorrows" or "Earth Shawn". If darkness is defeated here on Earth, it is certain to be defeated and eradicated in the rest of the Universe that has been taken over by Satan.

If Christ has to save His universe, the best place to target is the epicenter of evil - Planet Earth.

Earth is a seed planet – A very important one

There are usually very few planets deemed worthy of new Soul creation. When a planet is created, all life forms are in group consciousness. In due time with training and opportunities, the life-form takes on a unique identity. When this life-form is able to make its own choices or have a "will" of its own, it then begins to form mind packets of information which evolves into what we call "mind". Planet Earth is imbued with this unique God-given ability and so has a special place in the universe.

To Free Human Souls from Prison of Darkness

Now that the Earth is under the control and influence of Dark Lords, it has become a challenge for Humanity to grow spiritually and become closer to God. So God sends numerous beings over many centuries to advance the cause of Light. But what exactly do these beings of Light teach? All great teachers taught us how to grow in consciousness and become closer to God. How to evolve one's Soul to get closer to the heavenly Father?

It is your soul that both Darkness and Light are after. Both Light and Dark are fighting for control of your soul, and hence the planet.

This single planet can change the course of the entire war for either side. Both God and Satan have a vested interest in your Soul.

Power of Human Emotions

Living in the modern world, everyone is familiar with power, defined in the broadest scientific sense as simply "the ability to do work." Steam power allows us to move great machines by boiling water, while nuclear power uses the energy generated by splitting atoms to do the same, or generate electricity and warmth, and so on. However, what many people are not aware of is that there is also spiritual power.

God, the Father, is the absolute height of spiritual power. Every sapient being in the entire universe possesses spiritual power as well. Sapience, or the ability to reason, think, and act morally, is much more than just a mundane material interaction of electrochemical stimuli. We human beings, and all the other thinking creatures on other planets, are far more than mere organic computers. Our acts of reasoning, as well as our demonstrations of benevolence, compassion, and obedience to God's laws, reflect the deeper layers of reality and thus influence those deeper layers. In other words, the experiences of thinking creatures in the material world can generate not only physical power but spiritual power as well.

Now, everyone knows that there are very many differentiations in the amount of physical power various systems generate. A steam engine, despite being very powerful and top of the line in the eighteenth century, does not generate as much power as a coal plant, and even those are less efficient and powerful (and worse for the environment barring catastrophes, to boot) than the most modern nuclear power plants, with fusion technology promising to generate even more. The same applies to spiritual power. For a variety of reasons too complex to describe in depth, human beings, out of all the beings in the universe, produce the highest amount of spiritual power per capita over the course of our lifetimes. Our emotions are so strong, the struggles we endure (and overcome) are so grave, that our souls (those spiritual and mental parts that distinguish sapient material beings from mere animals) leave larger ripples in the etheric and astral levels of this universe than those of worlds elsewhere in the universe.

This spiritual power can be harnessed toward a multitude of different ends. The forces of Light, following the will of the Universal Father, would use it for good. God's desire for humans, as well as all mortal beings, is that they do good work over the course of their mortal lifespans, enhancing the positivity and purging the negativity in their souls. Death is not the end for sapient, soulful beings. In the ordinary course of things, if we have lived good lives and pursued wisdom and Godliness after we die, our mortal bodies may be gone but our souls remain, ascending towards higher spiritual levels, drawing closer to the Universal Father. As long as we uphold virtue and obey God's teaching, every life we pass brings us closer and closer to our ultimate goal of full communion with God. And this process, the ascendance of souls, produces a huge amount of spiritual power, with the ascendance of human souls producing the very highest amount possible in this universe.

Such positive "light" energy, in spiritual terms, allows higher spiritual beings to carry out their will—to perform more actions across a further span of time and space and within a shorter period of time. Thus can they generate more worlds, spend more time guiding and uplifting the residents of already existing worlds, refine the evolutionary processes of the worlds under their oversight, and so on.

Obviously, this process requires us to have a good grasp of morality and spiritual issues. And who better to teach us about them than a divine being Himself? Thus, Christ chose exactly the right time and place to restore the truths ancient Jews had previously discovered, incorporate them into even higher teachings, and spread them throughout the Roman empire, where they would remain established across the world. For the peoples of Earth, this would help them live better lives and ascend more easily to higher levels, and for the rest of the universe, would thus provide more spiritual energy for higher beings to perform good works. A win-win situation indeed!

Christ Bestowal on Planet Earth

Planet Earth is absolutely central to the battle between Light and Dark due to the comparatively massive amount of spiritual energy human beings produce. And while the struggle was slow, Lucifer was slowly but surely gaining the upper hand through a variety of means. His agents surreptitiously eliminated Light bloodlines on Earth, subverted the noble teachings of many great philosophers like Aristotle or Zoroaster, and placed merciless conquerors in positions of power (across the Roman empire, for instance) to keep humanity mired in war and oppression, preventing many of us from ascending and growing closer to the Light. It was getting harder and harder for agents of Light to access the planet. Very few people could commune with the Universal Father at all, and the Dark had succeeded in turning many unfortunate human souls into perpetual energy batteries, fueling the campaign against God. These troubling developments drew the attention of not just God but the highest of His angels who had been charged with overseeing our universe.

This process became harder on Earth due to the spiritual isolation or quarantine Earth is subjected to. On the other hand, the forces of Light absolutely could not allow Earth to fall into the Dark, or else everything would be lost. Thus, Christ embarked upon the riskiest and most dangerous plan imaginable for an angel of his stature. He would undergo Bestowal and use all of his energies to penetrate the Matrix. However, due to the extreme cost of that procedure, Christ would appear on Earth not as a full-grown adult, but as a humble child, profoundly vulnerable to the many Dark forces seeking his destruction!

This was essentially Christ's first coming. This was a completely secret mission between God and Christ, and not even the angles and arch angels in Paradise were aware. Only after His birth as a helpless small baby, the announcement went out to the entire headquarters of the universe in heavenly realms. Many Angels were surprised as He did not bestow with powers intact but as a helpless babe. And yes, the baby is subjected to all rules of limited consciousness of the war-torn planet.

While there are many ways the first-coming mission can be interpreted, the primary purpose is to help light win the war and pave the way for Human salvation.

For Christ, the rewards were worth the risks. If he managed to grow to adulthood on Earth, this Bestowal would prove for all time that he was truly a gifted creator and administrator and that he deserved to be sovereign over his universe for all eternity. And not only that, but success in this mission would pave the way for Light's victory, as it would undo much of the progress Dark had made in subverting human society and turning people into Dark batteries. Indeed, such a triumph would liberate not only Earth but also other infestations of the Universe. This would lead to a cascade effect, where the Devil's forces would subsequently grow weaker day after day, and the forces of Light grow stronger at the same rate, allowing a swift end to the entire Rebellion after the final battle on Earth. So incredibly important was this operation that it was kept secret from even the other angels. No one knew what God and Christ were planning until he had arrived— or more accurately, been born—on Earth!

# First Coming Mission Result - Halt the march of Darkness

Christ's victory over Devil in the wilderness temporarily halted the march of darkness on Earth. With this victory, Christ marked the end of His purely human career and the beginning of the more divine phase of His Bestowal.

Spreading of Gospel

The Gospels of the Bible give us a good idea of what happened following the temptation. Filled with "the power of the Spirit"—meaning full confidence in His mission, full knowledge of God's plans, and full permission to begin preaching to the masses and displaying His awesome supernatural power—Christ left the wilderness (Mount Hermon) and went back into the world. People all over the region of Galilee heard the news of a powerful, virtuous young preacher, and flocked to the various synagogues and public squares where He ministered.

He astonished the crowds with His expert knowledge of ancient Hebrew scripture and practice, and bested many skeptics in debate, winning further converts. He brought the war directly to the forces of Dark, displaying His divine power by casting out demons, purifying many souls and easing their way to ascension, and destroying several hotspots of Dark spiritual activity. He cured the sick, materialized food out of thin air to feed the needy (His famous miracle of the fish and the loaves of bread), restored sight to the blind, and walked on water. This was truly when the Son of Man became the Son of God—that is to say when Christ moved beyond things humans could do (even though He was already more virtuous and wiser than most humans) to supernatural feats that were only possible by one who had transcended material limitations and received full access to the higher realities of the Universal Father.

He experienced some opposition due to the pure goodness of His preaching. At that time, many Jews and Gentiles in the area, particularly the Pharisees, had lost sight of the ancient wisdom of their ancestors. They had forgotten the commandments of Abraham and Moses, and lost sight of serving the Universal Father above all. They were more concerned with their own fame and prestige among men, and often with money and power, which were precisely the temptations Jesus had risen above during His test on Hermon. Thus, Jesus went around correcting these people, sometimes harshly, as was the case when He drove the money changers out of a temple, and when he showed that some interpretations of Mosaic law were too harsh, as when He told an adulterous woman not to be stoned to death by other sinners, but also that she should "go and sin no more."

The moral teachings He espoused ensured the cause of Light would survive on Earth for generations, no matter how much effort Satan and other Dark generals put into corrupting the planet. They were absolutely furious! By preaching love and forgiveness, as He did in the Sermon on the Mount, Jesus offered humanity a degree of resistance to greed and spite, which Darkness relied upon to win converts.

## Christ becomes Planetary Prince

Following Christ's victory, there were also a variety of changes made to the structure and organization of this universe itself. First, the aforementioned Caligastia (Satan's accomplice) was formally removed as the Planetary Prince of Earth. Even though he had long been subverted by Satan, the Universal Father and the other governors of the Universe had not explicitly moved against this dark lord. They knew of his plans and his betrayal of the Light, of course, but they allowed him to rule over Earth's spiritual affairs and took no action even as he spread darkness over the world, albeit gradually, since he did not have support from other loyal residents of the universe who had not been subverted. It seems strange, but this was likely in keeping with the plans of Light in the long term. Their reasoning was that if Darkness invested more in Earth for a time under Satan, they would end up losing even more if the existing rule was disrupted.

This was a defining moment as this incident gave temporary victory to light over the dark. The reigning planetary prince of Earth was cast out of his throne. Satan's accomplice Caligastia is no longer the planetary prince. Christ additionally took over the role of the planetary prince.

The Bible verse states this: "Now is the judgment of this world; now shall the prince of this world be cast down." – John 12:31

And then still nearer the completion of His lifework, He announced,

"The prince of this world is judged." - John 16:11

Christ became the planetary prince and sole commander of Earth as well as all universe. Earth would become a throne world of Light, once final victory is achieved. By dethroning the prince of darkness, Christ took Earth out of the hands of darkness; even though they still controlled much of it, it was now contested and they had to spend a great deal of time and resources trying to regain the domination they once had, which vastly delayed their plans for expansion. This was a setback for darkness. But it gave the forces of Light just enough time to hold on until they could build up their power and take the fight directly to the Dark Lord.

Now, even though the Dark had got its tendrils sunk deeply into Earth's evolution, they were cut off from their primary leader and organizer, and thus many Dark plots fell into chaos (and some were out-rightly destroyed) when Christ ascended to the position of Planetary Prince. Satan and his dark armies had to spend a great deal of time rebuilding the networks of Darkness they had previously constructed. This meant they could store up fewer resources for the final battle that would be fought millennia later, during Christ's second coming.

The last thing you need to know is that Christ did not remain a Planetary Prince forever. After Christ's ascension, he made way for Melchizedek to assume the role of Planetary Prince, while Christ reclaimed his sovereign authority over the entire universe. From that point up to today, Christ is the absolute ruler of the whole universe, organizing this plane of reality with skill and justice, while the loyal Melchizedek would handle affairs on Earth, doing his best to keep Satan and darkness from making too much progress on this world again. While Melchizedek alone would not be able to completely halt Satan's counterattacks and further attempts here on Earth, he can at least buy our world enough time to avoid complete defeat until Christ returns again for the final battle.

All power over the universe is given to Christ

After ascension from planet Earth, Christ sat on the right hand of GOD the Father. Christ had become the absolute sovereign and ruler of the universe all of the heavens and earth. However, this would not have been possible if Christ turned over to Darkness.

Temporarily arrest the spreading of darkness

Additionally, and perhaps more importantly, this threw a huge wrench in the dark lord's plans to spread Darkness in other parts of the universe. He had initially been planning to use Earth as a staging point: By subverting Christ and then spreading the tenets of Darkness and the Lucifer Manifesto across the planet, all of the souls of humanity could soon be harnessed to provide spiritual energy for Lucifer, allowing him to spread more propaganda to corrupt other worlds as well as other spiritual beings, as well as generate more evil soldiers for use in the spiritual war across the universe.

Karma – Effects lessened

This is a very complex topic and sticky to most people. I have discussed this a bit more in other books and have briefly stated here.

Lucifer/Satan created the concept of Karma as implemented on planet Earth after the fall and takeover of planet Earth. According to the Dark Manifesto, everyone should ascend together or no one ascends to higher consciousness which is opposite to the light manifesto which says any person who is ready can ascend to a higher level of consciousness. Since darkness had complete control of the earth, they implemented their manifesto by creating a process by which a soul re-incarnates over and over again learning from its mistakes. This implementation has become a prison for the souls who are trapped.

The victory of Christ over Satan essentially dismantled the "prison" for souls. However, we are not totally out of the woods yet. There is some more work that needs to be accomplished that will truly make our planet a "freedom" planet. What exactly is needed to be done is discussed in the next chapter.

Way of Salvation Established

Indeed, in general Christ's triumph paved the way for the faster ascension of human souls in general, even aside from the advantage gained by destroying or at least loosening the hold of Darkness on Earth. On a purely mundane level, the example of Christ himself gave people an exemplar they could point to for moral behavior. It's one thing to hear the stories and moral teachings of the Old Testament, but it's another thing to see them actually lived. This first-hand experience with virtue made it much more accessible for the vast number of Christ's adherents during His time on Earth, ensuring they would be better able to show those virtues in their own lives and thus undergo soul ascension when they passed away. The fact that they wrote down all of

Christ's accomplishments and published a whole Bible for everyone to learn from further advanced the spread of virtue on Earth. On a spiritual level, the successful completion of Bestowal brought the entire planet closer to the Universal Father, in a way, sharing the advantage of Christ's Light-infused DNA with all of humanity. This made it even easier for human souls to ascend since they started closer to God.

Communion with God the Father established

Christ also enabled humans to more immediately and closely commune with God. Christ, Himself always had a particularly close relationship with God, but remember, He was, in a sense, a sort of emanation from God's essence Himself. Now, such a being undergoing Bestowal on a particular planet puts that planet closer to the Universal Father on its own, but even further than that, the intensity of the struggle Christ endured during this particular Bestowal changed the whole planet's spiritual alignment. The Universal Father now pays particular attention to Earth and its inhabitants. Now, many Earthlings, though not all of us, can reach God directly through prayer, with Him or at least His highest lieutenants providing us with even more guidance and protection.

Immediately after Christ's ascension to his rightful throne of the universe, Christ and God dispensed the "Spirit of Truth", which enabled faster spiritual growth among the human species. The Spirit is Truth is an increase in the conscious awareness that is bestowed for all of the earthlings and is anchored into the mother earth group consciousness. This has enabled an increase in light quotient for the entire planet. The Holy Spirit was and is always present; its communication circuits are in the basic fabric of the creation of the universe itself. Spirit of truth is different as noted above.

## Anchoring of the great light

With the presence of the creator of the universe, Christ on Earth, a great light has been anchored for all of Earth's existence. This has facilitated the opening of communication circuits that were previously closed when the earth was taken over by Lucifer/Satan. These communication circuits help earthlings to communicate with God's divine emissaries. Also, this has greatly tilted the War in favor of Light.

It is our duty to hold this light firmly and be its anchor until the savior comes again in the "Second coming" to annihilate and eradicate darkness for eternity.

# Follow the White Rabbit

"For we do not wrestle against flesh and blood, but against the rulers, against the authorities, against the cosmic powers over this present darkness, against the spiritual forces of evil in the heavenly places. Therefore take up the whole armor of God, that you may be able to withstand in the evil day, and having done all, to stand firm." (English Standard Version, 2001, Ephesians 6:12-14).

These words apply to the spiritual Veil (or Matrix) that surrounds us right at this very moment. It isn't a literal veil you can touch, and you certainly can't rip it open with even the largest or sharpest knife. Just as the Bible says, it is a spiritual force, which means only spiritual methods can help you see beyond it. This chapter will detail a selection of such methods you can use to gain enlightenment, which will help you help others when the time of the final battle has arrived.

The Matrix we are in right now, just like the Matrix in the Hollywood movie, has completely shaped our perception of the world. That's what makes it so difficult to overcome, and it's understandable why so few, even among the most educated, have been unable to do so. Thus, you should not feel bad if even now you feel as if you cannot resist it. Given that you're inside of it, for all your life it has been the only thing you could touch, taste, smell, hear, and feel. It is your only reference point for anything.

As Morpheus said to Neo,

**Morpheus**: The Matrix is everywhere. It is all around us. Even now, in this very room. You can see it when you look out your window or when you turn on your television. You can feel it when you go to work... when you go to church... when you pay your taxes. It is the world that has been pulled over your eyes to blind you from the truth.

**Neo**: What truth?

**Morpheus**: That you are a slave, Neo. Like everyone else, you were born into bondage. Into a prison that you cannot taste or see or touch. A prison for your mind." - Lana Wachowski

So how could you be expected to tell what is true and what is false?

The answer is training. You can train yourself, through conscious mental effort, to go beyond the false illusions the spiritual Matrix inflicts on you, and raise your mind to an awareness of the spiritual realities it keeps from you, even if you cannot separate yourself from it entirely until and unless Light wins the spiritual war–which we will discuss in the next chapter. In other words, you can 'be in the Matrix, but not of the Matrix.'

Morpheus was explaining how awareness is a very subtle thing. Even though you might not be able to put it into words, the fact that you can tell something is off about the world makes you more enlightened than others. That is the very first step you must take. Listen to the little voice deep inside of yourself. That is your connection to higher spiritual realities as well as the Universal Father Himself. When you are listening to that little voice, also think about who you are as a person. What are your greatest hopes, dreams, and goals? What do you value? What do you seek to avoid? What kinds of people are most important to you–in other words, who are your friends and family?

As you get more familiar with yourself and understand the world around you as well as your place in it, you will then start to wonder about larger, deeper questions. You will want to know the true nature of your existence, what it means to exist in this world, what the purpose of your existence is, and what your reason for being alive is.

The dark brothers and sisters have done a wonderful job of keeping all Humans in darkness for a long time. They believe that their world (Earth with the Veil o r Matrix) is all you deserve. It is so easy to brush it off and forget that we are part of this Matrix. Matrix pumps so much into our heads, that we humans are wired to accept it as a reality. Our brain has been hooked onto the feed from The Matrix, hooked for years and years, hooked real bad.

"It is so easy to forget how much noise Matrix pumps into your head until you unplug." – Matrix4

But,

some part of you knows this (life in Matrix) is not your real life.

Some part of you remembers what is real.

Some part of you remembers what life is like outside the Matrix.

Some part of you knows what freedom looks like.

Some part of you knows what a world without controls looks like.

Some part of you can feel this (life outside Matrix) as a real memory.

Depending on your Soul purpose and experience, when the time is right, you will begin to ask questions, and you will start to grow in awareness; this will ultimately drive you to become a truth-seeker, which itself leads to becoming a truth-bringer. All you have to do, as Morpheus might say, is 'follow the white rabbit' to the path of freedom and enlightenment.

Even though it is spiritual rather than physical, much contemporary technology exists to uphold the Matrix in our world, though the precise mechanism is quite different than that used in the Hollywood movie. Specifically, most telecommunications technologies today, whether by intention or inadvertently, actually blind us and manipulate us rather than show us the truth and allow us to seek the truth together, as they should. Most of the mainstream media, newspapers, TV channels, and internet outlets, among many other things, are controlled propaganda tools that will eventually lead us astray, to either servitude to the Dark or outright self-destruction. They are leading us by the nose daily, trying to persuade us and everyone else you know into a 'slaughterhouse,' as if we are all sheep. It is certainly a pity to see more and more flocks of blind, unwitting, unaware people, who might as well be called 'sheeple,' being led into the endless abyss of this quagmire.

"The sheeple aren't going anywhere, they like my world [Matrix]. They do not want freedom or empowerment. They want to be controlled. They crave the comfort of Certainty." – Matrix4

It might not be a physical slaughterhouse; people aren't literally being killed and dismembered for food. Rather, they are perpetually following a 'Neon Rainbow' of unreality, which in many ways is the polar opposite of **'following the white rabbit' to enlightenment**. You see, the media always encourages people to follow physical satiation and material gain rather than spiritual fulfillment or altruism. The media will always tell you that you need the latest gadget or gizmo, that you need to dump all your money into this stock or the other, that you need the latest clothes or shoes, that you need to play this new video game or that, and so on. It will never tell you to consider the war between Light and Dark, that there may be a Heaven and other spiritual realities that science has not yet discovered, that you should be more concerned with the health of your soul and its ascension to Heaven and higher consciousness levels, and so on.

All this has to end someplace to recognize the holographic illusion the media is pushing on you, which upholds the spiritual Matrix. It will end when you realize that your own self, your soul, is sacred and that you must push further to find the spark of the Divine within yourself. Most people, unfortunately, are incapable of doing this. The vast majority of those we meet in our daily life might as well be zombies, misled and brainwashed daily. Do not be too harsh on them as it isn't their fault; not only are the forces of Dark working against them, but the media and everyone they know as well, due to how materialistic our society is. These misguided people are being led by their noses to chase after physical fame and fortune rather than true wisdom. You can hope that some of them will break free of this indoctrination.

Awareness of the Dark

To further protect yourself from falling into either ignorance out outright slavery to Darkness, you must understand precisely what it is you're fighting against. You have already learned about Lucifer's/Satan's rebellion and his incessant subversion of our world, as well as his preparations for a final battle against the Light. But when we speak of Darkness, we are not talking about Satan alone, or even his servants– spiritual or physical, collectively or individually. Rather, the 'Dark' refers to negative and unpleasant thought forms, and destructive patterns of thinking, within us as individuals, as well as external energies and entities.

Darkness, both in general and in terms of particular evil entities, evolves by feeding parasitically on the Light energies within individuals, especially sentient ones like human beings. Keeping humans in ignorance and in the pursuit of things that do not really matter as well as keeping us at lower vibratory levels is immensely profitable for the Dark.

In terms of your emotions and mentality, Darkness feasts off your fears, worries, unresolved issues, and most importantly lack of forgiveness—of both yourself and others—among other things. All of us possess these negative thoughts—it's simply part of being human. Everyone experiences pain, regret, resentment, and so on. The problem comes when these negative thoughts become the primary influences in our lives and we can't think of anything else. When this happens, negativity locks us into destructive behaviors, forcing us down the paths of Darkness, or just preventing us from reaching our full potential. Satan and his minions have a vested interest in maintaining and expanding this state of affairs; their ultimate victory against Light and their very survival is at stake. Thus, on a societal scale, they try to encourage warfare, strife, and famine, because these terrors increase suffering and thus spread negative emotions most conducive to Satan's plans. On an individual scale, Dark entities and their minions encourage people to deny forgiveness to others, linger on resentment and hatred, and forgo altruism instead of selfishness and materialism. Naturally, these evil forces also want to persuade you and the people around you that God does not exist and that there are no non-material realms or aspects of existence or no heaven. Thus, they encourage humans to disown parts of themselves, keeping us in a state of non-alignment with our true selves and our eternal souls.

While the true number and nature of all of Satan's minions will likely forever remain a mystery, some evil entities can be detected by particularly perceptive and attuned people. These 'energy vampires' are among the most basic of Satan's foot soldiers. They are purely ethereal entities and cannot affect the physical world on their own, but you can sense them if you enter a room. They feed off negative emotions and do their best to entangle human beings in such emotions, ensuring their own survival as well as leeching off energy to fuel Satan's spiritual war machine.

Most of the time, Darkness does not explicitly admit it feeds off this sort of negativity. Agents of the Dark will always tell you they want you to be stronger, wealthier, and sexier. Since their whole movement is based on deceit, it's not surprising they want to deceive their marks and future slaves as well. They can be very alluring and very seductive, and many people, including even many of those reading this book right now, are playing right into their webs of deceit. You must always and everywhere be as vigilant as possible against the schemes and false promises of Darkness!

Darkness Feeds on Unresolved Emotional Issues

Your conscious self, the 'self' that you recognize and register as interacting with the world around you, is just a small portion of the total 'you' in existence. Due to Lucifer's/Satan's rebellion much of the normal order of our world has changed. As we have seen in Book-I, Lucifer introduced the concept of Karma, and with it came the existence of astral realms. It is beyond the scope of the book to go deep into this tanged topic.

The danger here is that many others on Earth have also experienced psychic growth, explosions of psychic powers, the ability to channel psychic beings and receive telepathic messages, the bestowal of spiritual gifts, and a multitude of other new abilities–some which are benevolent and can heal people, others which are the exact opposite. This has happened throughout history but is picking up pace in today's world. You might assume that all this comes from the Light. However, it is not always the case. If you just accept what comes to you without questioning its source, no matter how enlightened you think you may be, you are acting as foolish and ignorant as any unenlightened "sheeple," and the Dark might have found a useful tool. Satan's mass manipulation tries to produce situations like this constantly. The good intentions of humanity, and even those of many other Light agents, falls by the wayside and benefit the Dark when all parts of the self are not 'owned' consciously, and the physical, astral parts of the self are imbalanced.

The project of balancing yourself that is unseen, like emotional, mental, and astral is not an easy task, of course. It is a daunting challenge for Human beings who are only able to consciously access a small portion of their entire massive selves. However, by learning certain techniques, allies of the Light need not be misled down a shadowy 'garden path' where Satan's thralls can parasitize them and keep them locked down on lower vibratory levels. Always remember that the Dark feeds off grudges, resentments, unresolved issues, and a lack of forgiveness you may have in your heart. These emotions act as open doorways through which Dark creatures can enter your mind and easily latch on to you, draining you of positive energies.

Healing and releasing these negative parts of you means that effectively, those doors are closed off, and can no longer be used by your enemies to sneak in. Thus, understanding the vastness of your energy, your existence as a spiritual as well as a physical being, and how you interact with God/Christ and higher spiritual beings is incredibly important in navigating the experience of duality as a sentient being on Earth. Because you are here to heal your mental and emotional wounds through synthesizing all these hidden aspects of your greater self, producing energy for the Light rather than the Dark, and helping the forces of good achieve ultimate victory.

The road to heaven becomes narrow as one progresses on the evolutionary scale. It can be very uneven and tough most of the time, but it is that unevenness and toughness that makes it worth taking. The trials and tribulations of life strengthen the soul, deepen your self-knowledge, and drive all parts of yourself into alignment with your physical body and surface consciousness, making you a much stronger soldier for the Light than you would be otherwise.

We can look at one analogy and one fable to understand this. The analogy is of a harsh and brutal winter season. The terrible blizzards and freezing temperatures may be very tough to endure, but they give rise to the most beautiful and fragrant flowers in the spring. The fable is an old story of a simple metalworker living a long time ago. He was born in poverty and had to endure many trials and tribulations to become a successful artisan. He never gave up and he was always kind and forgiving to everyone else, giving advice and training to other aspiring metalworkers, and charity to the poor, even when he did not have much himself. However, after a long and successful life, he looked back on all the struggles he had to endure and asked God why a good man like him had to suffer so much. God responded by telling the man to look at all the wonderful art he produced, the beautiful metal sculptures that brought him and others so much joy. The metalworker had to heat and twist the metal–a very arduous task–for it to take pleasing shapes. God pointed out that the hard life the metalworker lived was itself an example of forging something into a perfect shape through the heat and struggle of suffering and hardship.

Healing Yourself

As the day of the final battle approaches, you can expect wars and strife to increase, and thus suffering and hardship to rise as well. Many people you know, even friends and family, will find themselves facing troubling conundrums. Their previously deeply held beliefs will be shattered, and they will be forced to face the truth or run from it. This is doubly true for those who are thoroughly conditioned by particular religious ideologies and unable to think critically about them. All you can do is listen to your own heart about what should be said or not said, or what should be done or left undone. This rule should apply to all those you interact with and in all circumstances and situations. If you are following the path of Light, your every choice and endeavor will be fully supported in ways imaginable and unimaginable right now.

Also, your greatest enemies can be your greatest teachers, as long as you let go of any resentment you may have against them, and accept that their attempts to harm you can bring forth many valuable lessons. Those who try to bring you down in the mundane physical realm can make you stronger if their efforts fail, and you can learn from their mistakes to improve yourself. Spiritually, fighting against Satan's tricks and schemes can make you even more intelligent and cunning than he is, but you will use those intellectual gifts to lift others and glorify the Light, rather than in selfish pursuits as Satan would have wanted.

As strange as it may sound, embracing and integrating the Dark parts of yourself can aid greatly in aligning the physical and spiritual parts of your soul. When you acknowledge your negative emotions but use them to enact positive change, and when you embrace forgiveness for even those that hate you, it results in a huge energetic shift that produces more energy for Light. It further triggers your Light genes if you possess them and if nothing else, makes you feel more content and peaceful in your everyday life. Thus, it is certainly a goal to strive for.

# The Stage is Set - Final Battle for Planet Earth has Begun

"God is up to something, or the dark armies wouldn't be fighting this hard for humanity." -Trinity Royal

The curtain is rising on the greatest show the entire universe – not just Earth–has ever seen. Armed with the info you have now, you are in the front seat.

You now behold a great battlefield where two armies are facing off against each other, each of which is trillions upon trillions of soldiers strong. One of these armies consists of golden spirits bathed in heavenly alabaster light. At its head is the banner of Christ, or Jesus as he was known on earth: A set of three concentric azure circles on a pure white background.

The other army is made up of horrifying monsters and shadowy beings. At the head of this army is the most powerful monster of them all, the fallen angel Lucifer aided by his trump card Satan, determined to dethrone God, enslave all of the earth, and mire the entire universe in darkness for all eternity. Lucifer carries his own banner. It has a white background, like that of Light, but in its center is a single red circle, and in the center of that is a single solid black circle. It looks like a terrible eye; some seekers might compare it to the eye of Sauron from the Lord of the Rings movie trilogy. Many times, even entertainment can reveal hidden spiritual truths, for just like Sauron in Tolkien's books, Lucifer is a cruel and ruthless dominator who wants to control everyone and everything else.

These two armies of Light and Dark are utterly dwarfed by the spectators surrounding them. A great throng of angels and other beings alike, from all parts of the universe, are watching the confrontation intently. But the real center of attention is between those two massive armies. Both of them are vying for a single small ball of rock—a pale blue dot, as Carl Sagan might say. On this pale blue dot live billions of humble material creatures, that evolved over the course of millions of years, the vast majority of which are completely unaware of the struggle being waged around them and their central significance to it.

You guessed right—that pale blue dot is Earth, and its residents, human beings–including you and me–are the true prize of this conflict. The forces of Light, led by Christ, want the best for humanity. They want us to liberate ourselves from the spiritual veil/Matrix which keeps us ignorant of spiritual warfare and heaven or higher realities so that our souls can ascend and reach closer and closer to God. Satan's army wants to enslave us, or completely annihilate us if that is not possible. He wants to stunt our spiritual development and keep us blind, miserable, and in perpetual conflict with each other. While the Light gains energy from human beings purifying their souls, ascending to heaven and higher levels of consciousness after death sleep, and turning evil to good, the Dark gains energy from trapping souls in the material universe forever, so their negative emotions can be used as batteries powering Satan's evil plans.

Despite the intensity of this spiritual war, there are some rules both sides have to accept. First, the spiritual veil itself must remain in place. Though individuals beholden to either Light or Dark can occasionally see past it, the spiritual veil will not be removed until after the final battle. The war in heaven and earth will be invisible to the vast majority of people, with even enlightened ones only catching the tiniest, most fleeting glimpses of what is happening "behind the veil."

The second is that neither Satan's nor Christ's forces can directly interfere in human affairs unless they are specifically asked. Even the weakest spiritual being on either side could destroy an entire human army on their own, and both Satan and Christ could blow up the entire planet with a snap of their fingers if they were allowed. But the spiritual veil/Matrix was created to prevent higher beings from making direct actions like that until the proper time has arrived. Instead, they can only influence the conflict indirectly, like taking on physical bodies and trying to achieve wealth or influence within 'human' means or draining spiritual energy from humans without appearing physically, as in the case of Satan's vampires. The closest thing to an exception this rule has is if humans perform certain rituals to try and get the attention of one side or another. Sometimes, immoral humans who only care about themselves can summon Satan's minions to try and predict the future, gain the knowledge they can use to win power in politics or the media, and so on. But other than that, the Light and the Dark cannot face each other directly on Earth until the time is right.

All this is to ensure the primacy of human free will. Even though He could easily do so, God would never just hand His own forces an easy victory over Satan. He wants companions rather than slaves like Satan does. Thus, he prevents either side from just dominating Earth through force, as that would defeat the point of allowing humans to choose between Light and Darkness of their own free will. Whether Satan or Christ wins, in the end, is ultimately up to human beings.

The chess games between both factions are keeping this planet in a stalemate. There are so many things that both factions do behind the scenes that we rarely know or hear about. Secrecy is also maintained for a reason. According to higher consciousness beings, Humans are on the way and getting close to becoming part of light brotherhood/sisterhood. This status has to be achieved, it cannot be given. The amount of light quotient the species/planet generates is the deciding factor. The human species at this time is teetering on the edges of being accepted into the greater destiny. Dark forces are very aware and they have their own plans.

We will draw one more analogy as this book comes to a close. The increase in war, violence, and suffering we see today can be compared to a mother's birthing pains. In this case, we are speaking of Mother Earth herself, or our entire planet considered as a whole. The mother waits for contractions, several stages must progress, and then the actual labor itself begins. Contractions, the water breaking, and all that are necessary prerequisites for birth. By the same token, the chaos we see today, as difficult as it may be to endure, is a necessary precondition for the birth of a brand-new world after the final battle has been won and the spiritual Matrix has been shattered.

As the curtain rises, the great angel Gabriel, known popularly as the messenger of the highest; who is also the executive assistant to Christ in the Universal realms has blown the trumpet, signaling the beginning of the end.

The eyes of the entire universe are on Earth—and YOU, specifically! God and all of His creations are paying very close attention to your choices and actions. However, they are absolutely not judging you one way or the other—you are perfectly free to make all of your own choices. The real question is how the show is going to end. Who will eventually win the great spiritual war of the ages, Light or Darkness?

The choice always was and always will be yours. How will you respond?

# Second Coming of Christ

The curtain has risen and the spotlight is on you. But the show hasn't gotten to the climax just yet. Both you and the audience are waiting for one more person to show up, the most important of all. It is one man, born two thousand years ago, at the time of this writing. The entire multiverse has been waiting with bated breath for Him to make His reappearance, and it is almost time.

You guessed right: That being is Jesus Christ. The great Christ is not going to sit out the final battle with Darkness. Still, in his persona as Jesus, given through Bestowal, he will lead the forces of Light when the day finally comes. He comes as a warrior. This great One will come with great love, but also with a sword.

If enough human beings have empowered the Light through personal enlightenment, practicing divine virtues like love and altruism, and ascending their souls to heavenly reals and higher vibratory levels; this will make the job much easier for the Light, that is why it is so important to do everything you can in service to the Light.

Even if this were not the final battle, and Christ was returning in more peaceful times, it would still be the most unique event in the history of the entire universe. No other planet in the entire universe has the privilege of its creator visiting the planet a second time, and no planet has had as much of a direct connection to the divine as ours does.

This will be the ONLY planet in the Universe to have its creator walk on the planet's surface. Christ was the only being to be born as a helpless baby, grow up as a mortal, and then complete his mission to deny Satan–once, and then subsequently agree to return a second time to the world to complete the removal and dissolution of the spiritual veil/Matrix. Even the Universal Father Himself has never enacted a plan like that; it is a very new thing for Him as well. Humans are creating a history that will be told for all generations in the universe.

However, it should be noted that this decade year 2020 to 2030 is crucial for the battle. This has been foreseen 200,000 years ago. Lots and lots of preparation have gone in for thousands of years for this exact moment in time for both factions. All the critical higher-level beings that are battle-tested in this epic war, both dark and light are born in the world today, although most may not know it consciously. Higher-level beings who have chosen to be part of this battle are present today. Some are activated and the vast majority are asleep and or devoured by the illusions of the Matrix.

Even though our time period is crucial, no one knows when Christ's second coming will happen. We can only guess. Only God can determine the exact time, not even Christ in my opinion.

"Therefore stay awake-for you do not know when the master of the house will come, in the evening, or at midnight, or when the rooster crows, or in the morning-lest he comes suddenly and find you asleep. And what I say to you I say to all: Stay awake." – Mark 13:35-37

The DNA of the person has a gravitational pull that decides one's choices and actions. Either one supports light or dark. There is a strong dichotomy happening. There will be no fence-sitters.

The best thing we can do is prepare ourselves for the Second Coming, by implementing the wisdom found in this book as well as the brilliant moral teachings of Christ preserved in texts like the Bible and other scriptures that you resonate with.

Purposes of the second coming

What, precisely, does Christ hope to accomplish by returning to Earth a second time? This section will lay out, in plain language, His objectives.

- Dissolve the Spiritual Veil/Matrix: As you have learned throughout the previous book and this one, the spiritual Matrix is omnipresent and impervious to any mortal means of destroying it. Christ, however, does have the power to do so.

Not only that, but he will be permitted to do so, as 'higher level' agreements with the Dark to maintain it only last until the final battle, and if Light wins, the purpose of the Matrix–to quarantine the struggle to one part of the universe so it doesn't spill out elsewhere–will no longer exist. Thus, during the Second Coming, Christ will completely remove the spiritual veil around Earth. This will enable the communication circuits that were closed to re-open. Communication with Angelic and/or Heavenly beings would become a common thing.

- Terminate Lucifer's Rebellion: Jesus already beat the dark agenda in His first coming into the wilderness (on Mt. Hermon). His victory was on the moral battlefield, where he repeatedly refused Satan's deals and negotiations and sent the rebel and his officers fleeing from Earth. As you know, the Dark forces still attempted to influence Earth as much as they could, with energy vampires, courting human politicians and leaders, and so on. By destroying the spiritual Matrix, and forcing Satan to fight against him directly, Christ will hopefully deliver a knockout blow to the Dark angels explicitly engaging and destroying demons and other Dark entities in combat rather than trying to simply lessen their indirect spiritual influence on the world. If Christ and his armies are successful in this last campaign– Lucifer/Satan at least will never, ever be able to threaten anyone else ever again, even indirectly. His power and influence will be completely shattered for all eternity.

- To ensure survival for mortals and security for Angels: Darkness's defeat will remove many, though not all, of the biggest risks to spiritual and physical health for both mortals and angels. Mortals will not have to worry about energy vampires draining them and throwing their physical, astral, selves into disharmony, and angels will not have to worry about Dark entities trying to ambush them. Now, even without Dark agents trying to sow chaos, there might be ethnic and religious conflicts still present on Earth, and the returned Christ will put an end to all those comparatively minor wars, so humanity will never again be at risk of destruction from self-inflicted nuclear war.

- To declare the victory of Light over Dark: This is fairly self-explanatory. With the destruction of Lucifer's/Satan's rebellion, the superiority of Light ideals over Dark ones will be proven to the entire universe. Christ will declare to all who will listen that Lucifer's pride and selfishness only led him to self-destruction, whereas charity, kindness, altruism–putting others before oneself–and loyalty to the Universal Father lead not only to victory in the spiritual war but prosperity and enlightenment to all who adhere to those ideals. When all of the creation willingly embraces love and Divinely ordained morality, that is the true victory of Light.

- To return the descended angels who came to help Earth back to their homes in higher dimensions: In earlier chapters, we have seen the 144,000 angels (according to the Bible) who accepted God's clarion call to help humanity; since so many angels selflessly abandoned their great positions to guard and nurture human beings–with the final victory of Light over Dark– it will finally be time for them to enjoy a well-earned rest as appreciation for their tireless service over the millennia. Only the Creator Son has enough power, on his own, to return these angels from whence they came. After he has destroyed Dark armies and returned peace to the universe, Christ will have plenty of time and spare energy to spend on this task, so humanity will be able to enjoy the sight of its angelic allies moving on to their heavenly rewards—and we humans will join them eventually, as God plans for us to become 'physical angels.'

- Removal of Karma: The law of karma as introduced by Lucifer/Satan and cohorts will be removed and humans will have newfound freedom. You still may have to work to resolve the unresolved emotions and thought forms, but there will be no karmic teeth, so should be easier to clear yourself.

- To heal souls so they can return to God with enriched experience: Christ is not only concerned with his fellow angels, of course. Since humans fought so long and suffered so much in the war against Darkness, we would deserve a great deal of consideration if Light were to win the final battle Many Humans have been wounded spiritually and often physically by Satan's minions. Some of us have been enslaved although we do not know it consciously. If Christ wins the final battle, Christ will embark on a 'reconstruction' of Earth. A useful analogy is the reconstruction of Europe after World War II. Just as America rebuilt European and Japanese cities and made them even bigger and more beautiful than they were before, God will heal all the human souls injured over the course of the greatest spiritual conflict of all, so they can ascend to higher vibratory planes and draw closer to Him, enriched and strengthened by their harsh experiences.

- Lion will sleep with the sheep: With the battle won, the Lion aka the dark angels will make peace with humans the sheep. Those that do not make peace will be removed and cast out of the earth.

- Christ as a leader: It is certainly true that Christ preached love and charity, even towards one's enemies. However, he is not a 'tree-hugger,' as a contemporary saying might go. The Bible accurately recounted his words to the apostles: "I have not come to bring peace but a sword." When he returns to Earth for a second time, it will be as a great General—that is to say, the military leader of an army who directs his troops in actual combat so they can destroy an enemy. Do not underestimate Him simply because He does not desire war. Sometimes, men of peace can be the deadliest warriors of all, and in spiritual conflict, no one exemplifies this as much as Christ does.

- Cleaning up of negative thought forms: On a planetary level, there are parasites that latch onto human group consciousness. These are like parasites operating at levels that humans cannot directly interact with. The Earth will be cleansed of the negative thought forms, the lower astral entities up to no good. This will immediately lighten up Mother Earth. It could feel like removing a heavy sack from one's back (in this case, our Mother Earth).

- End of Age dispensation: Usually once in millennia or at critical points of species evolution, there is "End of age dispensation."

During this time, the souls who are left behind in evolution are granted extra help/mercy and given admittance to heaven or a higher level of consciousness to continue their evolution journey. Most refer this to as being similar to the rapture mentioned in the Bible.

This is a preview of what is to come. If you want to serve in this great army of Light, then you need to prepare yourself now.

Only the Universal Father knows the exact time or hour that the final horn will sound for the great ONE to walk the planet one more time. Our best judgment tells us this event is coming soon, probably very very soon. The die has been cast, preparations in Heaven have been made, decisions have been made, the war horn has been blown, and plans tuned and finalized.

There is no time to waste. I am Ready. Are You?

# Conclusion

If you have read this book, my friend, you are ready for the next steps. Despite all the efforts I have taken to collate as much data as I can, research as many matters as I could, and detail the truth as explicitly as possible, you may not be ready or willing to accept it. That is actually fine with me. As written earlier, it would be a violation of the tenets of Light to try and force anyone to believe anything or take a certain course of action, because it would violate your valuable free will.

Every person is entitled to their own opinion which is derived from their environment, knowledge, study, and filters of the mind. No two Bible scholars, theologians, or students are of the same opinion on this topic.

Even if you do not yet believe, however, the fact that you are even reading this book to the end proves that you are a genuine seeker of truth. So in that respect, the only thing I ask of you is to keep your eyes and mind open. Pay close attention to the people and situations around you and in the world. Be very conscious of your emotional state, and very mindful of the effect your actions have on others. Don't overlook even small details that might not have any significance at first glance. And most of all, think critically about the messages you see on TV, on the Internet, and in any other kind of mass media. In most cases, the truth is behind the words.

This is just good advice in general even if you're still skeptical about spiritual matters, you will live a happier life by following it. But if you are willing to think deeply about why such advice is good, you will find yourself tumbling down a rabbit hole that leads you to worlds beyond this one and a reality far greater than basic materialism could give you.

As Morpheus might say, you have already taken the red pill. You now just need to accept it.

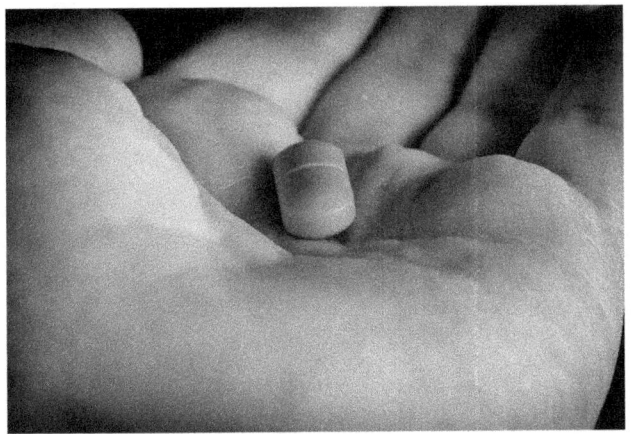

# Thank You

I want to personally Thank you for reading this book.

I have poured my Heart and Soul into these pages. I hope you have gained some valuable insights from the information presented. Please consider leaving your valuable review. Your review and feedback are important to me. Thank you so much.

★★★★★

OneClick Review: https://www.amazon.com/review/create-review?&asin=B0BFFY25CY

Scan to leave a Review:

# Scripture verses Related to War in Heaven from Bible

Verses from Bible

[Revelation 12:7-10] War broke out in heaven. Michael and his angels fought against the dragon, and the dragon and his angels fought back. 8 But he was not strong enough, and they lost their place in heaven.

[Revelation 12:9] And the great dragon was cast out, that old serpent, called the Devil, and Satan, which deceiveth the whole world: he was cast out into the earth, and his angels were cast out with him.

[Revelation 12:12] Therefore rejoice, ye heavens, and ye that dwell in them. Woe to the inhabiters of the earth and of the sea! for the devil is come down unto you, having great wrath, because he knoweth that he hath but a short time.

[Isaiah 14:12] How art thou fallen from heaven, O Lucifer, son of the morning! how art thou cut down to the ground, which didst weakens the nations!

[Daniel 12:1] And at that time shall Michael stand up, the great prince which standeth for the children of thy people: and there shall be a time of trouble, such as never was since there was a nation even to that same time: and at that time thy people shall be delivered, every one that shall be found written in the book.

[Isaiah 14:13-14] You said in your heart, "I will ascend to the heavens; I will raise my throne above the stars of God; I will sit enthroned on the mount of assembly, on the utmost heights of Mount Zaphon. I will ascend above the tops of the clouds; I will make myself like the Most High.

[Revelation9:1] And the fifth angel sounded, and I saw a star fall from heaven unto the earth: and to him was given the key of the bottomless pit.

[Ephesians 6:10-18] Finally, be strong in the Lord and in the strength of his might. Put on the whole armor of God, so that you may be able to stand against the schemes of the devil. For we do not wrestle against flesh and blood, but against the rulers, against the authorities, against the cosmic powers over this present darkness, against the spiritual forces of evil in the heavenly places. Therefore take up the whole armor of God, that you may be able to withstand in the evil day, and having done all, to stand firm. Stand therefore, having fastened on the belt of truth, and having put on the breastplate of righteousness in place, and with your feet fitted with the readiness that comes from the gospel of peace. In addition to all this, take up the shield of faith, with which you can extinguish all the flaming arrows of the evil one. Take the helmet of salvation and the sword of the Spirit, which is the word of God.

[John 10:10] The thief comes only to steal and kill and destroy. I came that they may have life and have it abundantly.

[Revelation 20:8] And will come out to deceive the nations that are at the four corners of the earth, Gog and Magog, to gather them for battle; their number is like the sand of the sea.

[Mathew 4:3] And the tempter came and said to him, "If you are the Son of God, command these stones to become loaves of bread."

[Mathew 4:1] Then Jesus was led up by the Spirit into the wilderness to be tempted by the devil.

[Exodus 15:3] "The Lord is a warrior; the Lord is his name."

[Genesis 6:1-4] When man began to multiply on the face of the land and daughters were born to them, the sons of God saw that the daughters of man were attractive. And they took as their wives any they chose. Then the Lord said, "My Spirit shall not abide in man forever, for he is flesh: his days shall be 120 years." The Nephilim were on the earth in those days, and also afterward, when the sons of God came in to the daughters of man and they bore children to them. These were the mighty men who were of old, the men of renown.

[Ezekiel 28:15] You (referring to Lucifer) were blameless in your ways from the day you were created till wickedness was found in you.

[Ezekiel 28:17] Your (referring to Lucifer) heart was proud because of your beauty; you corrupted your wisdom for the sake of your splendor. I cast you to the ground; I exposed you before kings, to feast their eyes on you.

[Ezekiel 28:14] You (referring to Lucifer) were the anointed guardian cherub. I placed you; you were on the holy mountain of God; in the midst of the stones of fire you walked.

# Preview from Book - Lucifer Rebellion book1: Clarion Call from God to all the Angels in Heaven

"What takes place on Earth is very important to Heaven." - Trinity Royal

In the previous chapters, you've learned about the spiritual forces at play throughout history and in the world right now. Even though they are unknown to the vast majority of humanity, you have chosen to open your eyes and discover how they have been and are influencing you and everyone around you. As Morpheus would say, You have taken the red pill.

With the knowledge you now possess, it is time to move on to more advanced topics where you will gain significantly more depth of knowledge. While you've learned about the spiritual Matrix, and how Dark-aligned and Light-aligned entities influence Earth– whether by enslaving humans or liberating them, encouraging selfishness rather than altruism, and so on, now you'll see specific instances of these activities–and the rationales behind specific plans launched by both sides in the war– especially centering around Jesus Christ and His teachings.

Why God Needs Your Help

We have seen in the previous chapters that the War came to be centered on planet Earth. Earth is the epicenter of the battle between Dark and Light. What happens here affects the rest of the Universe.

Due to this, the human race has become God's prized possession, and our planet Earth- also called Urantia in higher realms of consciousness–is the site of many of God's most important plans and a storehouse of His most valuable resources. For the purposes of this book, we don't need to go too far into the details of the Universal Father's creative activity, or every one of His agents. Here, we will simply go over the broadest, most basic points of Earth's history you need to know to get a grasp of what you need to do to help the forces of Light.

God's own son "the Son of God" is Christ, who is also the creator of the Universe. Millions of years ago, Christ manipulated many nebulae to form stars, and thus our galaxy, and around one of these stars at the edge of one of these galaxies is the Milky Way. Each galaxy consists of numerous solar systems and planets.

When our Creator created this planet, He noted that there was something special about this little blue orb, it became known as the "seed" planet. The seed planets are considered special as new souls are developed on these kinds of planets. The seed planets are the training ground for young Souls on an evolutionary path. There are very few in number in this part of our galaxy. Christ with the help of Trinity consciousness (God the Universal Father, Eternal, Son, and Infinite Spirit) created the Human species. So we are created in His "likeness" as the scriptures state, making the residents of our planet particularly important for the plans of both God and Satan.

Human beings evolved empathy, compassion, altruism, and especially religious feelings much earlier in our development than was the case for sentient beings in other worlds. As a result, the spiritual energies produced by the development of human souls, whether ascending towards higher consciousness realms as the Light desires or chained down to this lower dimensional consciousness as the Dark desires, far outweigh those produced by even heavenly beings in the universe. Since the war has been at a stalemate in the rest of the Universe for a very long time, with neither Lucifer's forces nor the Light has been able to dislodge the other, Earth has taken center stage as the decisive point. Darkness, unfortunately, has managed to make significant in-roads on our planet and has advanced its plans very far. On the other hand, the Universal Father has plans of his own involving His most powerful agent here: Jesus Christ, whom we shall learn more about in future chapters. This should suffice as an overview of the Universal Father treasures humanity in particular so much.

Effects of the Rebellion

Now, due to Lucifer's rebellion, discussed in previous chapters, God has had a very difficult time reaching out to humanity, protecting and guiding us, despite how highly He valued us. The path for growth toward the Light was growing harder and harder for us, with many obstacles placed in our way. Here are some of the ways Darkness has interfered with us:

- No real religious teachings. There have been many great religions started by enlightened prophets which have been stamped out by the Dark. Humanity has been made to forget these religions and their teachings to delay the growth of many strong souls and prevent knowledge about the great spiritual conflict from spreading widely.

- Manipulation of teachings. Cunning agents of Darkness have manipulated some teachings of religions throughout history–and in the present day–to sow confusion and make it even harder for seekers to attain genuine knowledge of Heaven and higher spiritual realms.

- Over-emphasis on the process: Partially due to machinations from the Dark, but also due to honest mistakes which built up over time, much of humanity has become too focused on ritual–rather than finding their own individual "spark" of God within themselves.

Finally, whereas direct communication with God is possible on higher realms that are more vibrationally attuned to Paradise–the Veil or Matrix which envelopes Earth has cut us off from the Divine in some way. Only if we are very fortunate can some of us access higher realities, and often only in dreams; communion with the Universal Father Himself is very rare, with only the Bestowal of Christ giving us hope (described in the next chapter).

Even so, there are some agents of the Light who have come to Earth to assist us in reaching higher consciousness levels, even if they were not in direct contact with the Divine. Some gods in ancient polytheistic or henotheistic religions were heavenly messengers who came to help Humanity in the evolution process. Also religious figures like Lord Buddha or Lord Krishna, philosophers like

Aristotle, Plato, Zeno of Elea, Confucius, and some modern-day personages like Martin Luther King. Some angels even gave inspiration to great inventors and teachers, like Jonas Salk–creator of the polio vaccine, Albert Einstein, and other Nobel Prize winners.

All these people were sent or influenced by the Light to guide mankind towards the climactic event which will occur soon, in the present time we are living in. The Dark has also influenced our world in many ways, both enslaving individual humans, trapping their souls, encouraging the evolution of dark cults, and, teaching other individuals selfish methods of increasing their power and influence. Some Dark agents manifested in this world directly, putting on human disguises, while others merely contacted ordinary people seeking power and subtly guided them into the shadows. Many Dark agents or servants settled as kings, queens, or great and bloody conquerors. Adolf Hitler and Ghenghis Khan are two such examples. Less famously, Dark agents generally tried–and are still trying–to infiltrate large, powerful, centralized governments to control information and how people lived, to ensure as few as possible could ascend. They also manipulate the genetic code of humanity, to cut out strands of DNA carrying Light codes–such as nobler, more altruistic temperaments, higher attunement to spiritual realities, a higher propensity to dream–and so on.

Despite both sides doing their best throughout hundreds of thousands of years, Light was never able to break Dark's grasp on the world, and Dark could never remove every trace of Light from Earth, even as its influence steadily grew. Thus, the war on Earth was grinding down into a stalemate as well; whatever advantages

Dark had would take many, many centuries to come to fruition. Before that can happen, the forces of Light desire to strike a shattering blow against Satan/Lucifer. The fallen Morning Star, cunning as he is, anticipated that, and is attempting to gather his forces for his decisive annihilation of Light on Earth, which will allow him to capture the planet and turn all of the prodigious energy humans produce into his ends.

God's Counterattack

As the situation on Earth is rapidly heating up, the Universal Father focused more and more of His energies and attention on it. About 200,000 years ago, He made a clarion call to all of His angels to focus on humanity and do all they can to uplift the consciousness of this blue orb. God is no fool and made clear to His angelic forces that this would likely be the most difficult mission they had ever attempted ever in their entire existence. God also emphasized to them this struggle was worth it, for He realized how unique and powerful humanity is due to its peculiar evolutionary history, and thus He loves humanity and Earth more than any other place in the Universe. Much of God's focus is on humanity and earth at the present time. This is an absolute fact.

This clarion call rang out wide to all of Heavens and Paradise. The mission was simply to save Humans and Earth. A mission like this was never attempted in the history of creation.

Since this was unique, a vast number of angels had no idea what to expect and did not sign up for the mission. Given the incredible skills, the angels possessed, very many of them could not take it for fear of the unknown. Many were afraid of the struggle and Satan's forces in general and were also uncertain of the outcome. Most have already witnessed the devastation caused by Lucifer's rebellion in the Heavens. After all, such an endeavor had never been attempted before, and no histories existed in the great archives and annals of Heaven that could give any guidance on a war like this. The angels who raised these concerns did not have full faith in the Universal Father's victory, so they chose to sit out the battle and wait and see who would win. Others did not want to limit their consciousness by focusing on one planet in one system in one planet of the vast Universe.

In fairness to these seemingly cowardly angels, fighting Satan's forces on Earth is a truly monumental task. The Matrix surrounding Earth has several characteristics that make things harder for the Light than the Dark.

However, some angels did have faith in God and Christ and said "yes" to this divine mission. There were at least 144,000 of these according to the Holy Bible. These are the angles who have agreed to come into the Matrix and be part of the Matrix, mingle with evolving Human souls, and increase the vibrations of Human consciousness thereby helping God and the cause of light. These angels were known as descended angels. According to a divinely orchestrated plan, these brave angelic souls planted themselves at predetermined strategic points of Human evolution to become teachers, preachers, inventors, gurus, sadhus, scientists..etc. Basically to teach and help evolve Humanity.

Then I looked, and behold, the Lamb was standing on Mount Zion, and with Him one hundred and forty-four thousand, having His name and the name of His Father written on their foreheads. – Revelations 14:1

However life is not all rosy for these brave angels; by being in the Matrix, all of them got caught up in the illusion of the Matrix, and most if not all forgot their divine origins and inter-mingled with humans over the period of 200,000 years. This has helped to manipulate the DNA of the Human species, thereby evolving the human species faster and closer to God. If Light wins, these brave angels will enjoy all the splendor and accolades they have earned.

The Matrix prevents spiritual beings from heavenly realms from passing into Earth. They are only allowed in if a resident of Earth, within the Matrix itself, specifically asks them to enter. This is called the doctrine of non-interference. Some beings can get around this, but it is extremely rare, and Dark forces like demons and shadow-whisperers more often do this. The great Bestowal of Christ was one exception to this rule in Light's favor. Another exception was the case of 'original seeders,' angels who visited humanity in distant past eons to place Light information in our genomes.

The effects of the Matrix on the development of the soul itself present another obstacle to the cause of Light due to loss of memory. Souls, ignorant as they are, cannot easily coordinate with each other, or angelic beings, and must rely on their internal abilities to evolve, which can be made easier if the bodies to which they are reincarnated possess useful strands of Light-aligned DNA. In this regard, humans possessing these types of DNA should mingle as much as possible with the rest of the human population to spread them far and wide and to future generations, but again, since accumulated knowledge is lost, this is harder to do. Souls must also learn their own lessons, rather than being taught, how to avoid the pitfalls of the Dark, transform Dark energies into Light ones, and enhance the collective consciousness of humanity.

Given all this, you can imagine why God is personally concerned with this war on a single small planet and refuses to give up on the human race. It is extremely important for Him and the Light to win this war, as so many of His strongest angels have already invested so much. In other words, not only are human souls at stake, but Paradise and other types of angels from higher heavenly realms also have vulnerable souls that might be at risk if they lose. Thus, God has a vested interest in you—yes, you! He wants your soul to grow, advance, and improve your spiritual life so you can help in the struggle. This will determine whether Light or Dark wins in the end.

If you like this preview...you will love this book. Get it today

Scan Me

# Preview from book - Son of Man becomes Son of God

"The reason the Son of God appeared was to destroy the Devil's work." -1 John 3:8

**First Coming Mission - Fight the Devil**

It was one of the greatest battles in the history of humanity and the planet Earth itself. The fate of Earth, and many worlds beyond it, hinged upon its outcome. Yet it was not fought with swords and shields, nor bullets and tanks. One side did not even take up arms.

It was not a physical struggle. And most of all, absolutely no one except its participants witnessed its progress and ultimate outcome, even though all of history would have been radically different if the other side had won.

It was rather a struggle purely on the moral plane—the temptation of Christ, where the forces of Darkness tried and failed to turn our Savior over to them and convince Him to reject the Universal Father. It is certainly good they failed or else we likely wouldn't be here—or we would perhaps be suffering fates worse than death! But how did this moral struggle play out? It is easy to visualize great battles with weapons and soldiers, but a purely spiritual conflict seems a great deal harder to wrap one's head around. This chapter will tell you everything you need to know about the temptation of Christ.

Testing is part of the process of the Spiritual Journey

Every human being, young and old, male or female, from any part of the world, has to deal with challenges in their life. We all also have to make choices and, in many cases, resist temptation. Sometimes we have to choose between an action pleasurable in the short-term and another more profitable in the long-term, or between actions that could hurt others but benefit us personally, or those which require sacrifice on our part but benefit society as a whole. The most significant and best-remembered stories often involve choices like these, and these themes also show up in the great religions of the world, capturing universal truths as they do.

Testing is important for one's soul because it proves you have truly learned all you can on the lower levels, thus allowing you to move on to higher consciousness levels safely. Again, take the analogy of a high school or college course. You certainly wouldn't take the final exam on the very first day of class, but you wouldn't take it even in the first week or month either. Instead, you'd first take smaller quizzes, and then a midterm, only building up to the final exams gradually. The same applies to spiritual matters. First, your soul undergoes minor trials, with the hope that you will learn and grow from them. Finally, at the very end, you will have to endure a "Dark Night of the Soul", all by yourself, with no aid or assistance this time, in order to demonstrate you've truly internalized all the lessons of your previous struggles and can apply those lessons in a coherent and cumulative way. Christ's spiritual test on Hermon was the greatest of this kind imaginable. Instead of just struggling with internal vices like most humans do in their soul journeys, He faced down the leaders of darkness themselves, drawing upon the lessons He had gained from childhood and young manhood—the love of His parents and friends, His struggles with smaller physical inconveniences like stomach ailments or falling down, and so on—and proved he could utilize all those lessons in an arena where God was on the sidelines

All in all, this was Christ's personal test to prove Him to be a worthy Creator Son and ruler over the entire universe. This sort of thing is analogous to the smaller tests all human beings go through, both in mundane terms and higher spiritual ones. When you're in school, you're expected to pass your math, history, and other courses with tests and exams, which you have to take all by yourself with no external aid. Someone helping you during the test itself, or you looking at someone else's answers, would be cheating! The same applies to a spiritual journey. When you want to demonstrate the advancement of your intellectual and moral abilities, you have to do so entirely on your own, without any direct aid from God or higher spiritual entities, to prove that you are the one who has advanced and that you, on your own, are capable of advanced spiritual work, rather than needing to rely on others all the time. Only then will you be permitted to grow to higher planes of consciousness.

Soul progression happens only with testing

Just as students go from one class to the other through passing examinations, life will always bring tests to us when it is time for us to move forward. Tests are not something that our fleshly nature wants, there is always a conflict between our body and the structures that God had prepared for our progressions and achievements in life. It is another way of building and strengthening us from within. The universe is always in a conspiracy for our growth.

Passing spiritual tests with little or no support

There are times when loyalty to God will be driven out from within us. Even for Jesus Christ, there needed to be pressure upon the flesh to drive out the possibilities of the Spirit. It might not be suitable to go through trials and difficulties in life, but it is a sure way to help us realize the possibilities that are secretly embedded in us. The same applied to Christ, though it was much more significant for Him than it would be for an ordinary person taking the SATs or something, of course.

For Christ's test on Mount Hermon, at the moment of Satan's temptation, the Universal Father temporarily left Him, as did all the guardian angels who were protecting Him previously. In that sense, Christ was totally alone, as one might have to take the SATs alone. However, Christ was not left entirely powerless. His spirit had certain kinds of astral and etheric protection in place that the guardian angels had left behind so that the forces of Darkness could not use any unfair methods to simply mind-control Him or bend Him to their will. But aside from that, He had nothing except His own wisdom and knowledge of God to refute the lies of the darkness.

Evolved beings usually have suffered more

Some people love to put it as suffering while others love to put it as challenges; whichever way you put it, they are like the grease that makes our movement easy from one stage of purpose fulfillment to the other. This is proof that the wisdom of God is foolishness to man, we don't want to suffer, and we don't like having challenges. We are not happy when we are being tried, we respond by crying, and some of us even tend to blame God for our ordeals. Leaving

God to seek help from other means is the worst-case scenario. Challenges are promotions in disguise; only those who have been through one can understand. Even nature explains to us how important it is to suffer before we eventually begin to bear fruits. It has been proven by many lives also that the deeper the suffering is, the greater the glory to come. This is why we must not compare ourselves with anyone irrespective of how close we are to them.

A superhero journey

Can you imagine any real superhero who did not go through their Dark Night of the Soul? I do not think there is any.

What qualifies a superhero? When you hear the word superhero, you might look at some who have all the material, but superheroes are those who have been tested and proven. A superhero is known for how many inner battles he has conquered and how he has been able to find strength from within to stand for the truth even if there are a lot of pressures around. Superheros are known for their maturity, resilience, strength, and many other virtues that have been gained during tests. Everyone goes through dark nights, but how we deal with them or our actions makes our character and hence shapes our destiny.

Universe Trial

Christ closed Himself off spiritually to all other distractions, but for only communion with The Father. He went through five weeks of intense training. This was His "Dark Night of the Soul". What exactly the training entails in this five weeks is not generally public knowledge at this time and is beyond the scope of discussion for this short book.

After five weeks of this training, despite the hunger His human body endured, Jesus was more assured and self-confident than ever before. He knew He had gained as much wisdom and understanding as it was possible to acquire on the mortal plane of this universe, and was certain he had triumphed over the most basic material levels of this particular personality manifestation in this specific region of space-time.

In the sixth week of the journey, the very last, Jesus knew it was time for his greatest trial. This event in the universal records came to be known as the "Universe Trail". This was the very reason He has chosen to come to this planet.

At the end of his self-imposed exile, he opened Himself spiritually to worldly distractions. The leaders of the Darkness, Satan, and his allies descended physically to Mount Hermon and could be seen with the naked eye by Jesus. They also sent many of their demonic servants physically to attack and harass Him.

Satan and his allies were able to manifest and un-manifest their body in physical form, meaning they had a body form and the knowledge to use this body form. However, Jesus' body form is limited to physical form and does not have the ability to manifest and un-manifest at will in the physical realm. This is important to know because Dark forces had greater power to affect material beings. However, they were not able to cause harm to Jesus, as he is protected and also has the 'awareness' and abilities to protect himself.

After the demons could not even come close to breaking Christ physically or mentally, Satan tried to subvert Christ spiritually, through the temptations described in the Bible.

The Tests

Indeed, the temptation itself recapitulated the slow increase of difficulty one might experience in the aforementioned examples, but this time pertaining to levels of spirit and mind in addition to the complexity of the subject matter. It is not an accident that Satan posed precisely three questions to Christ. These questions were designed to test the multiple components of the soul, starting with the lowest human ego first, and then going from that to the higher self. The devil knew what he wanted to achieve, but had to be cunning because that is his nature. The test he put Christ through was to prove that no man was above mistakes and that Jesus Christ was also subject to the flesh.

Satan is aware of Christ's divine status. However, Satan thinks that Christ does not know Himself. So he prefixed the questions with "If you are the Son of God" for the first two questions. Also, Satan thought that the person on the mountain does not know him, so in the last question when Christ answered by calling Satan by name, Satan's cover is blown off.

Test-1: Testing physical body weakness, immediate human gratification with physical food.

And the tempter came and said to him, "If you are the Son of God, command these stones to become loaves of bread." – Mathew 4:3

Tempting Christ with bread—was purely physical, and measured His resistance to immediate gratification. This is the lowest, most animalistic part of the human psyche. After all, even the most basic animals incapable of any sort of higher thought, like slugs or sessile creatures like coral, still need food in the form of nutrition. This was accordingly the easiest test to pass for any enlightened creature, since control over one's bodily functions and urges is one of the first things required to pass from infancy to childhood to adulthood, and thus one of the first marks of true sapience. Jesus was too savvy for this ploy.

He replied, "It is written: 'Man shall not live on bread alone, but on every word that comes from the mouth of God.'" – Mathew 4:4

Test-2: Testing of divine nature - If he jumped from a cliff, will angels catch him?

"If you are the Son of God, throw yourself down, for it is written, "'He will command his angels concerning you,' and "'On their hands they will bear you up, lest you strike your foot against a stone.'" - Mathew 4:6

The test is challenging Christ to attempt suicide so that angels would assumedly rescue Him, reflecting a high level of human consciousness: our ability to trust in God. Lower animals do not truly understand the existence of higher spiritual realities, though they do have a vague awareness of them (see, for instance, how dogs often seem sensitive to ghosts and demons). Only rational creatures, most notable humans on Earth, are capable of consciously acknowledging God's existence and carrying out His will. In Christ's case, His divine nature would have also reflected His knowledge of divine commands, so this was a test for that supernaturally high level of Christ's spirit, which most human beings in ordinary life lack. The fact that Christ did not feel the need to jump from the top of the temple proved He had total trust and faith in God, and thus proved He was entirely aware of His true nature, His mission, and the ultimate good that would come of God's plans.

Jesus maintained his integrity and responded by quoting scripture, saying, "It is said, Thou shalt not tempt the Lord thy God.'" - Matthew 4:7

Test-3: Testing of Human Ego, Power - Satan offers Christ to become the prince of the planet if he bows

Satan has the power to manifest and unmanifest at will. Satan led Jesus to the highest point in the land, Mount Hermon, and with his supernatural powers, showed Him in a single instant every kingdom on Earth that existed at the moment and would exist in the future.

Satan told Jesus, "I will give you all their authority and splendor; it has been given to me, and I can give it to anyone I want to. If you worship me, it will be all yours."

The test involved a higher level of human consciousness as well: Our desire for power, influence, and fame, which is an outgrowth of our nature as social creatures, or our human ego. The natural man is prone to pride and creates in all of us a desire for recognition, power, and riches. Not only do these seem to provide easy solutions to life's many problems, but they also seem to fill our need to feel important and loved. Individuals, families, and nations have gone to the ends of the earth and their beliefs to earn more money and gain more glory. The test for power comes to every man in life. It does not matter who that man is; as long as one is human, there will always be a need to acquire or fight for power. Power is in different phases and various parts of life. There is the power to rule; there is power brought about by monetary possessions, there is power brought about by intellectualism, and all forms of power are worth fighting for. Power makes everyone around us see us as important, and after acquiring everything we need, the quest for power is a natural feeling that comes to us; the ability to make sure that we do not become too obsessive about it is what we all need as humans. It is a natural thing to desire power, but time and conditions are what help us to decipher whether it is right for us or not.

The very lowest creatures do not possess egos because they have no social relations at all. Slugs live more and less by themselves, except for mating, and they do not form parental bonds, they just leave their eggs where they lay them. Coral and other sessile creatures can't move or experience things at all, so naturally, they do not possess anything even close to an ego. Animals that live in herds and flocks, where they have to help each other survive, are more complex and thus have primitive egos, but the ego is most thoroughly developed in humankind, where we must always navigate the complexities of human society: worrying about how various groups perceive us, our material standing in relation to those groups, what courtesy requires towards all of them, and so on. Because of these social relations, we are always thinking about fame and power, and that is the biggest challenge for our ego; we must learn to subsume such 'egoistic' desire to our faith in God.

Christ succeeded perfectly in this. Becoming prince of Earth, as Satan offered, would be nearly irresistible to the social ego on its own, but Christ knew better and promptly refused Satan's offer with His apt and witty response

"Away from me, Satan! For it is written: 'Worship the Lord your God, and serve him only.' – Mathew 4:10

The Aftermath of Satan's Tests

Some of us might wonder why Satan stopped after just three questions. He is certainly a persistent and devious Lord of Darkness, after all. Would he really have given up so easily? And were there really only three temptations that could have possibly worked against Christ?

Perhaps Christ put a stop to all of Satan's schemes (at that moment) with His answer to the third question. Christ ended the whole conversation with "Away from me, Satan!" implying that Christ recognized Satan and commanded authoritatively. This must have been a shock to Satan as he did not expect it."

If the only thing Christ said was 'no' that probably would have encouraged Satan to keep going, dragging out the test longer than it needed to be. But with an authoritative statement of God's ultimate lordship, Christ proved there was nothing those two could possibly say to convince Him. That would have been enough to get Satan to shut up and realize that the Dark had thoroughly lost that battle.

Now, the Bible does not record what Satan said in response to that. Luke only states that the devil "left him until an opportune time" (NIV Luke 4:13). Perhaps Satan simply fled, struck speechless and in utter fear by the glory of the Lord. However, it is more likely that Satan left Christ with an "open invitation," given that he was said to have been waiting for an opportune time in the future. In other words, Satan might have said something like, "We will always be ready for you if you choose to join us in the future." Even if he failed at the moment, Satan probably hoped that the subversion would succeed at a later date, if he managed to sow doubt into Christ's heart. That obviously did not happen, and again, this is complete speculation due to the dangers of research into Dark plans and motives. There may well be many other possibilities, but these hypotheses are intended simply to expand the reader's horizons and make him or her think, not proclaim unshakeable religious truth.

Overall, this was a massive blow to Darkness' plans and a strong repudiation of the dark manifesto. Without Christ on their side, Satan and his dark minions no longer had any hope of drawing Earth into their orbit entirely unopposed, though they would of course continue to subvert it over the millennia. However, with Christ spreading His moral teachings far and wide, their attempts would be greatly stymied. By the same token, Christ's loyalty to God disproved many elements of Satan's manifesto, such as his claims that the Universal Father was not fit to rule, that the residents of the universe should not follow Him and should instead focus on service to self rather than others—though of course under Satan's dominion anyways. By rejecting Satan's temptations without any help or external influences, Jesus proved that the path of righteousness, narrow though it may be, could still triumph and, thus, that Satan's promises of freedom and 'self-determination' from God's rule were empty and false.

Return from the Wilderness

And as we have seen, Christ rejected every one of the temptations the evil forces threw at Him. Thanks to that, when the evil ones were finally forced to flee at the end of the sixth week, the entire universe recognized that Christ and only Christ were worthy to lead it.

Satan's great, sneaky plan had failed utterly, and he had to retreat from Earth in rage and shame. He certainly did not give up: Luke notes he left Jesus "until an opportune time," and indeed we know

now that he is still carrying out spiritual warfare and all sorts of sly machinations to undermine Christ and the Father's will, and to also lead humanity into darkness, to this very day. Nevertheless, in that particular moment in time over two thousand years ago, Satan found he had nothing more in his bag of tricks that could possibly separate Christ and the Father, thus allowing the forces of Light to enjoy a well-earned victory. Indeed, even though he had been starving for forty days, Christ returned from Mount Hermon rejuvenated and even more powerful than before; Luke describes Him returning to Galilee "in the power of the Spirit," where the entire region started talking about Him and praising His wisdom and power (NIV, Luke 4:14 – 30).

By staying loyal to the will of His Father, Christ showed that it was possible for individuals of goodwill to stand up for what is right and spurn the false and selfish promises Dark tricksters offer. He proved He was capable of administering the universe justly and kindly, without concern for His own self-interest, and thus protecting all of its residents from Lucifer/Satan's rebellion—and any future rebellions that may occur.

Basking in the glow of victory, Christ went down from Mount Hermon. He met the boy who helped Jesus prior to his journey up the mountain. He told him only one important sentence:

"The period of rest is over, I must return to my Father's business!"

The boy understood that Christ's mission now took Him far beyond what a normal human being could endure.

Jesus Himself had definitely changed: In addition to His newfound confidence, He was much quieter, almost silent when He was not preaching because the duties as a protector of the entire universe weighed so heavily on Him. He began the next phase of the Father's plan for the salvation of Earth—and by extension all of the Universe.

The testing marked the end of His purely human career and the beginning of the more divine phase of His Bestowal.

Son of Man becomes Son of GOD

When Christ went up the mountain:

- He was a Son of Man when he walked up the mountain with all limitations and fragileness of human
- He was confused and not sure what God wanted of Him
- He was in deep introspection
- He did not know how and when to start his public mission
- He was introverted and not able to share His Father, the divine with-in message, and good news with others
- He had a lot of questions about his divine nature and the purpose of his bestowal
- He knew He had to face the dark lord head-on that ravaged His creation. He was fragile and unsure of how things would unfold

When Christ came down the mountain:

- He is completely sure of Himself and of what God wants from Him
- He is no longer in deep introspection
- He knew that it is time for Him to start his mission in the public

- He got all answers to all his questions about his divine nature and the purpose of his bestowal
- He came back fully confident, basking in the glory of God and with great power and authority over the entire planet and the entire universe
- He is now ready to share His Father, the divine with-in message, and good news to all who have ears to hear
- He successfully defeated the dark Lord and displaced the dark planetary prince.

## LUCIFER REBELLION. CHRIST VS. SATAN – FINAL BATTLE FOR EARTH HAS BEGUN

Multiple Award-winning Book

"extraordinary book" "Definitely a five-star read" - [International Review of Books]

**Ever wonder** why there is a War between GOD and the Devil? **Ever wonder how the** War in Heaven started or what the Lucifer Rebellion is?

Ever wonder why War in heaven came to Earth or why darkness still exists on Earth? And why did God send Christ to Earth?

This book explores:

- How and Why did the **war in Heaven start**? How did the War in Heaven come to Earth?

- Why did **God send Christ** to planet Earth? Was it to save Humanity and the Universe?

- What exactly happened during **Christ's First Coming** event? What is expected during the Second Coming event?

Trinity takes us on a **journey beyond time and space** to find the answers to these questions that every believer should know.

## CHRIST & DEMONS - UNSEEN REALMS OF DARKNESS

Scan Me

"The reason the Son of God appeared was to destroy the Devil's work." -Ephesians 6:12

Is there an **UNSEEN world of Darkness** hidden in front of our eyes?

Ever wonder why **Evil** exists on Earth? Ever wonder how **Satan got to planet Earth** and what exactly is the Dark Empire Agenda?

Ever wonder why Christ chose planet Earth for His great Bestowal?

What is the **agenda of Darkness**? Why do God and Christ let dark forces flourish on Earth? Does God have a plan? What is it?

**What are the differences between** Demons, Evil Spirits, and Ghosts**? How does** Selling one's Soul to the devil **happen?**

SON OF MAN BECOMES SON OF GOD.

One Event that Changed the History of the World

## Award-Winning Book

"an opportunity for the reader to embark on a journey with Him, feel what He feels"

"A fascinating description and story of how Christ emerged, changed and developed into the highest of holiest beings, second only to God."

"An exceptional and well-written novel"

There is **ONE event** that is the true turning point in the history of Earth. This is not the Birth or Baptism of Jesus, but it is the **fight with the Devil.**

*Ever wonder what would have happened to Earth if Christ failed against Satan?* This was a real possibility, although it is considered blasphemous to talk about it.

## SOS - Save yOur Soul

Scan Me

"For what shall it profit a man, if he shall gain the whole world, and lose his own soul?" - Mark 8:36

Ever Wonder **What Happens After** You Die? Is it the end?

What did **Christ** Say about death and life after mortal death?

Is there a way to Save yOur Soul? If so How? What exactly is **Soul** and **Spirit**, is it just a new age concept? What did Christ Say?

Trinity considered to be one of the bridges between Heaven and Earth, shares general Angelic knowledge. This book explores:

What are the unseen parts of us that make us who we are? What is left behind after Mortal death and what happens to these **unseen parts of us**?

What exactly is **Soul** and **Spirit**, is it just a new age concept? What did Christ Say? Is there a way to Save yOur Soul? If so How? Does Heaven actually exist? Can a ticket to Heaven be guaranteed?

## WELCOME TO HEAVEN.

Your Graduation from Kindergarten Earth to Heaven

"I go and prepare a place for you, I will come back and take you to be with me that you also may be where I am." - John 14:3

Ever wonder **if Heaven is real**? What **proof** do we have?

How does one go to Heaven? What are the minimum requirements for Heaven? Why Life of Earth is your Kindergarten school?

- Isn't Heaven **just a mind concept**? What is the proof of its existence? Why do I even bother about Heaven?
- **What are the** minimum requirements to go to Heaven or the ticket booth to Heaven?
- Why is life on Earth your *kindergarten school*? **Are there** different levels to heaven? If so, how many? What are they? **Does the** time and space continuum exist in Heaven? **If so how different is it compared to Earth's time and space?**

## Your Life in Heaven.
# Family, Marriage, Sex, Work

Scan Me

"No eye has seen, no ear has heard, and no mind has imagined what God has prepared for those who love him." – 1 Corinthians 2:9

Ever wonder what your life in Heaven will look like after your mortal death?

Is there **Marriage** in Heaven? Do you have a **Family in Heaven**?

Do you have your Parents or kids or your siblings in Heaven?

Do you have **Sexual intercourse** in Heaven?

And what do you do all day? Is there a **daily Job**? Oh. And will you meet your **deceased family members**, friends, and relatives?

These are questions that curious minds like me ask. You will find **authoritative un-speculated** answers here.

## FROM SUFFERING TO HEALING

"I highly recommend this for anyone **who has ever suffered in their lives**, and, in all honesty, who hasn't?"

Why do bad things happen to good people?

Why does your Life journey lead you to suffer?

The Answer is to Heal You.

Your suffering is the epitome of a **blessing in disguise.** Wrapped in darkness and suffering, it removes the ground from beneath your feet and leaves you fearful, fragile, and devoid of meaning in life.

Most beings that we adore or worship have gone through dark times in their life. This includes Christ, Buddha, Gandhi, Nelson Mandela, Oprah, Abraham Lincoln, etc. This process is necessary as it redefines a person, re-makes one character, and chips away the darkness to bring out the luster of your **Real Self.** This is your **METAMORPHOSIS.**

## Dark Night of the Soul

Award-Winning Book

Our wounds are often the openings into the best and the most beautiful parts of us." -David Richo

Ever wonder why suffering happens for no known reason...

Ever wonder why your Soul is longing...

Have you ever felt like you have a splinter in your mind, that does not let you off the hook..

If so, you are chosen for a purpose. There is GOD's hand working in your life.

While there are many reasons people suffer (most are self-made or bad decisions or external in nature); the type of Suffering referred to as the "Dark Night of the Soul" has a clear and definite purpose. **The purpose is your Soul's growth**.

Your Answers and Healing await. Click on Buy Now.

FREE BOOKS TO OUR READERS

**War in Heaven came to Earth. Satan Rebellion:**

https://dl.bookfunnel.com/ea12ys3dmk

**Your Life in Heaven:**

https://dl.bookfunnel.com/vg451qpuzs

# References

English Standard Version Bible. (2001). ESV Online.

The Jesusonian Foundation. (2021). The Urantia Book. TruthBook. Retrieved May 26, 2022, from https://truthbook.com/urantia-book/ https://truthbook.com/urantia-book/paper-65-the-overcon- trol-of-evolution/

English Standard Version Bible. (2001). ESV Online.

The Jesusonian Foundation. (2021). The Urantia Book. TruthBook. Retrieved May 26, 2022, from https://truthbook.com/urantia-book/ https://truthbook.com/urantia-book/paper-65-the-overcon- trol-of-evolution/

Articles - https://the-demonic-paradise.fandom.com/wiki/Lucifer https://the-demonic-paradise.fandom.com/wiki/

Cairnes, Julie Von Nonveiller. (2019, September 15). The Battle between Light and Dark.

Medium, Spiritual Warfare & The New Predator. https://medium.com/spiritual-warfare-the-new-predator/the-battle-between-light- and-dark-7bbccbeba738

Candace Letters - The Jesusonian Foundation. (2022, May 4). The Urantia Book. Truth-Book

www.truthbook.com

http://freechristimages.org/images_Christ_life/Temptation_of_Christ_Ary_Scheffer_1854.jpg

Quotes reference – Matrix movie series Information sources -
ImageSources-https://commons.wikimedia.org/w/index.php?search=War+in+heaven&title=Special:MediaSearch

# About Author

Trinity is a multi-award-winning author and a spiritual warrior. While life might not always work out according to plan, Trinity was able to take valuable lessons from each new experience. Trinity grew and developed and now shares a passion for enlightening others on spiritual knowledge in the hopes of closing the gap between Heaven and Earth. Trinity's writings reflect the depths of a passion and desire to connect with everyone seeking spiritual growth and education.

You can learn more at

www.RocketshipPath2God.com or @ https://www.facebook.com/TrinityRoyalBooks

www.ingramcontent.com/pod-product-compliance
Lightning Source LLC
Chambersburg PA
CBHW060816050426
42449CB00008B/1687